LSDerailed

Scott M. Davis

Purpose In The Pain Publishing
St. James, MO

© **Copyright 2021 - All rights reserved.**

The content contained within this book may not be reproduced, duplicated, or transmitted without direct written permission from the author or the publisher.

Under no circumstances will any blame or legal responsibility be held against the publisher, or author, for any damages, reparation, or monetary loss due to the information contained within this book, either directly or indirectly.

Legal Notice:

This book is copyright protected. It is only for personal use. You cannot amend, distribute, sell, use, quote, or paraphrase any part, or the content within this book, without the author or publisher's permission.

Disclaimer Notice:

Please note that the information contained within this document is for educational and entertainment purposes only. All effort has been executed to present accurate, up-to-date, reliable, complete information. No warranties of any kind are declared or implied. Readers acknowledge that the author is not rendering legal, financial, medical, or professional advice. The content within this book has been derived from various sources. Please consult a licensed professional before attempting any techniques outlined in this book.

By reading this document, the reader agrees that under no circumstances is the author responsible for any losses, direct or indirect, that are incurred due to the use of the information in this document, including, but not limited to, errors, omissions, or inaccuracies.

CONTENTS

Foreword	7
Author's Note 2.0	15
Introduction	21
1. KNOWNS OF THE UNKNOWN	25
2. INTO THE RABBIT HOLE	33
3. THE BEGINNING OF THE END	37
CHAPTER THREE PT.2	50
CHAPTER THREE PT.3	69
4. MY APOCALYPSE	79
5. REAPING THE WHIRLWIND	101
6. ONE LIFE	113
7. A MOTHER'S PERSPECTIVE	119
8. TREACHERY	125
9. WITHOUT AN ANCHOR	133
10. SHIFTING GEARS	145
11. AFFIRMATION	151
12. GLORY, HONOR, POWER AND PRAISE FOREVER, AMEN.	161
13. ALL JESUS	179
14. BROTHER AND SISTER SCOTTY DAVIS	185
Afterword	213
About the Author	221

Copyright © 2023 by Purpose In The Pain Publishing Inc.

All rights reserved. No part of this publication may be reproduced, distributed or transmitted in any form or by any means, including photocopying, recording, or other electronic or mechanical methods, without the prior written permission of the publisher, except in the case of brief quotations embodied in critical reviews and certain other noncommercial uses permitted by copyright law. For per-mission requests, write to the publisher, addressed "Attention: Permissions Coordinator," at the address below.

Purpose In The Pain Publishing Inc.

www.purposeinthepain.net

Publisher's Note: This is a work of nonfiction. All accounts are based on true stories. With the exception of changes in minor details for privacy reasons.

All scripture quotations are from the Authorized King James Version Bible.

Ordering Information:

Quantity sales. Special discounts are available on quantity purchases by corporations, associations, and others. For details, contact the "Special Sales Department" at the address above.

LSDerailed: Crashing Into the Occult; Train Wreck Turned Testimony / Scott M. Davis. — Expanded Edition
ISBN: 979-8-218-12149-5

FOREWORD

I first became acquainted with "Pastor Scotty" after Darren, a young man who had been attending the church I serve as pastor, was incarcerated in the Eastern Reception, Diagnostic and Correctional Center in Bonne Terre, Missouri. I was so excited to read the first letter Darren sent from prison that mentioned Pastor Scotty by name, and it was obvious that his ministry was having an incredible impact on his life. He was able to minister to Darren on a level I could have never achieved, and his powerful testimony was the key that set him free. Who would have thought that God would have already had an imprisoned apostle strategically placed and ready to take Darren under his wing? Truly God is a God who still answers prayer!

Today Darren is out of prison, reunited with his wife and five children, and serving the Lord with all his heart. He is an incredible husband, loving father, and passionate disciple of Jesus Christ. He is currently pursuing the ministry and sharing his powerful testimony to anyone who will listen. He often expresses how thankful he is that God sent him to prison so he could encounter Pastor Scotty's ministry.

Pastor Scotty continues to minister, and has now written his first prison epistle, that looks past the initial high of recreational drugs, and exposes their danger and negative impact on all those who fall prey to their influence. He also reveals the sinister power working behind the scenes that is not just destructive but deceptive. His unvarnished and powerful personal story is both a warning to the wayward and a message of hope for those held captive by the oppressor and fear there is no way out. Through the power of the Almighty Name of Jesus, another David has fought his Goliath and won, and now uses that same weapon that was formed against him to set at liberty anyone who wants to be free. Thank you, Pastor Scotty, for being so transparent with your testimony and contagious with your faith. Be encouraged and keep writing, for what the Apostle Paul said in his second letter to Timothy is still truth… "Although I am imprisoned, the Word of God cannot be chained." Amen.

Brother Chuck Carr
*Pastor of West Point Pentecostal Church
in Doniphan, MO, as well as District Secretary
of the UPCI Missouri District*

To all who've endured

As well as to my beloved wife, without whom you would not be holding this book in your hands. Thank you so much for all your hard work baby!

For to him that is joined to all the living there is hope:

for a living dog is better than a dead lion.

— ECCLESIASTES 9:4

AUTHOR'S NOTE 2.0

It is with great honor, as well as indescribable joy that I am able to present you with *the rest of the story*. When writing the first edition of *LSDerailed*, it was my conscious intent to avoid writing a "Christian book." I wanted to be able to get the book into secular rehabs and other places that would not give Christian literature a chance. I wrote it as though I were writing to myself at seventeen, and at that particular time in my life, I wouldn't have dared read anything with the label, "Christian" attached to it. So I did my best to *become all things to all men*, and accomplish the seemingly impossible task of telling my story without shouting the NAME above all names. But if *LSDerailed* was rated E, *Crashing Into*

The Occult; Train Wreck Turned Testimony is unapologetically rated JESUS! Amen? Amen.

For me this edition is so much more than a book. It is my soul bled out onto paper. It is evidence that the Father still runs to the prodigal, and the LORD of heaven still reigns sovereign in the affairs of men. It is the power that has delivered me from the jaws of the dragon, and the grace that has kept me through the darkest of my nights. It is why I live, and if necessary, why I will die. Accompanied by the precious blood of the Lamb, it is that by which I overcome—the word of my testimony.

In formatting this special edition, I have decided to leave the original text as it pertains to my personal story undisturbed, and add the new content to the back of the book. Beginning with a brief summary of my childhood and teen years, these extended chapters will hone in on what was actually going on during my deranged journey home. Having been thrown headlong into the abyss of evil, I will be sharing some firsthand knowledge into the powers of darkness that are currently sinking their sin-sick claws deep into the soul of our culture. I'll be taking you on an even stranger ride than before, but ultimately, I'll be revealing the nail scarred hand that through it all has never let me go. If you don't already know Him, I'll be introducing you to the Main Character of not only my story, but the Main Character of all creation's story—the One who chose me before I was ever conceived in my mother's womb, and the same One who loves you more than you could ever know.

It is my deepest and most sincere prayer that the truths contained in this book would become as real in your life as they have in mine. As you read, I pray your faith will be strengthened, and your courage renewed in the fact that there are no depths to which King Jesus will not reach to pull one of His own from the fire. Above all, I pray a special anointing upon all who read, that you would be permanently placed in the body of the resurrected Christ. Now let the redeemed of the LORD say so and let the gates of hell never prevail against the church of the living God. Amen, and In Jesus' MIGHTY name, Amen!

ORIGINAL AUTHOR'S NOTE

LSDerailed has been in the making since 2012, when I was arrested after a night of extreme paranoia and tragic violence. My passion for writing this book is simply aimed at wanting to educate and hopefully spare others from the tragedies my own victims have experienced. Along the way, I believe all who enjoy reading will be captivated by the stories I share and want to share this book not only with those they think it can help but also with anyone who enjoys reading in general.

My experimentation with hallucinogenic drugs has been fairly extensive, and along the way I have had some very unique experiences. Some of these experiences led me to believe these drugs were the "secret to the universe," while others drug me through sheer terror, caused severe damage to others, and ultimately landed me with a twenty-five year prison sentence. It's all scenic routes and smiles til you realize the train has gone off the rails, and you're not the only one aboard.

I have changed some of the names for privacy reasons, but other than that we will stick to the script. It is my sincere hope that the hard-fought battles you are going to read about can serve to benefit not only you, but our culture as a whole.

DICTIONARY

Trip - Common term used to describe one's experience while under the influence of hallucinogenic drugs

Peak - The most intense window of time during a psychedelic trip, usually occurring 2-4 hours into a twelve hour or so trip

Come down - The brain straining stretch of time commonly associated with the ending of a psychedelic trip

Persistent Psychosis - The clinical diagnosis for someone who continues experiencing the side effects of LSD use long after the actual use of the drug

Acid - Slang term for LSD

Hit - One dose of LSD

Ketamine - Animal tranquilizer, commonly used as an anesthetic by veterinarians, A.K.A. Special K or K

PCP - Formaldehyde or embalming fluid

Shrooms - Psilocybin Mushrooms

INTRODUCTION

What enjoyment is there in life without challenge? Every competitor who has ever lived, who has ever possessed one ounce of integrity, knows it is more enjoyable to lose ten games by one point than to win all ten games by one-hundred points. It is the challenge that keeps life interesting and propels us to improve. It stimulates thought and creativity, opening doors into the depths of our potential. We as human beings were born to struggle, to fail, to learn, to conquer, to grow—to be challenged and to overcome.

How many of us have become unfortunate pacifists in this all-important struggle? How many of us have slipped into apathetic laziness, and as a result, watched our dreams, goals, and desires float off into the monotonous abyss of what could have been? More importantly, why do so many of us succumb to this less-than form of existence? Is it the propaganda and subliminal influences that bombard us from the time of our earliest memories? I'm sure this along with many other contributing factors plays a major role in our complacent settlement, but I also believe there is something much deeper at work. Perhaps, despite our deepest desires to grab life by the reigns and witness our goals become reality, there is also an insidious and integral part of the human makeup that is bent toward sabotage and self-destruction. To untangle all of this would take an entire book of its own, but for now, may we simply address the nature of this innate war and understand that it is within the human mind that these battles are fought.

The apex of creation, the human mind is a powerful thing. It is a place of unfathomable beauty, as well as extreme danger, a place of limitless potential, as well as limitless destruction. It is the instrument from which we project not only our own perception of reality, but also the one from which we help to shape the reality of others. It is a fragile warzone in which the very manifestations of life and death are determined.

In thirty-two years of living, one of the greatest lessons I've learned is understanding that my words and my actions do not just affect me and my immediate surroundings. Far from the initial point of impact, the ripple effect of our decisions can alter the lives of people we've never even met before. I'm not sure we can readily understand the magnitude of such a concept, but even an elementary grasping of it should be enough to prompt us to actively engage in the war of our thoughts. For the mind that is not actively engaged in this fight is passively destroyed. So here's to the fighter.

1

KNOWNS OF THE UNKNOWN

LSD (lysergic acid diethylamide), first synthesized in 1938, is an extremely potent hallucinogen. It is synthetically made from lysergic acid, which is found in ergot, a fungus that grows on rye and other grains. Because of LSD's extreme potency its doses tend to be in the microgram (mcg) range, a typical dose ranging between 75 and 150 micrograms (millionths of a gram).[1] This is about 3,000 times less than the amount of aspirin in a regular-strength tablet. Because LSD is made illegally, and the potency is so great, there are often large differences in the amount of drug administered throughout different batches, making it very easy to accidentally take a larger dose than intended.[2]

LSD is thought to produce its characteristic hallucinogenic effects via interaction with the serotonin receptors in the brain. Serotonin is a neurotransmitter that helps control your behavior and mood, governs your senses, and moderates your thoughts.[1] LSD induces a heightened awareness of sensory input that is accompanied by an enhanced sense of clarity, but reduced ability to control what is experienced. The LSD trip is made up of both perceptual and psychic effects.[3] The user commonly experiences impaired depth perception, along with a distorted perception of time, sound, touch, color, shape and size of objects, movement, and even their own body image. Sensations may seem to "cross over," giving the feeling of hearing colors and seeing sounds. These side effects can be frightening at times, resulting in thoughts and feelings of extreme terror. This panic can then lead to the fear of losing control, fear of insanity, and even the fear of unavoidable death.[1]

When taken by mouth the physical effects of LSD usually include the drug initially being felt 30 to 45 minutes after ingestion, peaking at 2 to 4 hours, and lasting 12 hours or longer. Intravenous (IV) route will produce a much quicker reaction, usually within 10 minutes. Effects may include:

- dilated pupils.
- rapid heart rate, increased body temperature, and raised blood pressure.
- distorted perception of depth, time, sound, and color.
- impaired sense of touch, taste, and smell.
- irrational laughter.
- anxiety, fear, and depression.
- grandiose thoughts.
- hallucinations (mental, visual, auditory, physical).
- inability to rationalize.

Based on years of scientific research these are some of the basic conclusions we as a people have come to understand about LSD and its effects on the user. Unfortunately, however, there is still much we do not understand, nor can we. This is due to our lack of understanding the human mind—the instrument upon which the LSD plays.

For cognitive scientists, the word "mind" refers to that part of each of us that embodies our thoughts, hopes, desires, memories, beliefs, and experiences. The brain, on the other hand, is an organ of the body, a collection of cells and water, chemicals and blood vessels, that resides in the skull. Activity in the brain gives rise to the contents of the mind. Cognitive scientists sometimes make the analogy that the brain is like a computer's CPU or hardware, while the mind is like the programs or software running on the CPU... Different programs can run on what is essentially the same hardware—different minds can arise from very similar brains.

It is difficult to appreciate the complexity of the brain because the numbers are so huge that they go well beyond our everyday experience (unless you are a cosmologist). The average brain consists of one hundred billion (100,000,000,000) neurons. Suppose each neuron was one dollar, and you stood on a street corner trying to give dollars away to people as they passed by, as fast as you could hand them out—let's say one dollar per second. If you did this twenty-four hours a day, 365 days a year, without stopping, and if you had started on the day that Jesus was born, you would by the present day only have gone through about two thirds of your money. Even if you gave away hundred-dollar bills once a second, it would take you thirty-two years to pass them all out. This is a lot of neurons, but the real power and complexity of the brain (and of thought) come through their connections.

Each neuron is connected to other neurons—usually one thousand to ten thousand others. Just four neurons can be connected in sixty-three ways, or not at all, for a total of sixty-four possibilities. As the number of neurons increases, the number of possible connections grows exponentially.

For 2 neurons there are 2 possibilities for how they can be connected
For 3 neurons there are 8 possibilities
For 4 neurons there are 64 possibilities
For 5 neurons there are 1,024 possibilities
For 6 neurons there are 32,768 possibilities

The number of combinations becomes so large that it is unlikely that we will ever understand all the possible connections in the brain, or what they mean. The number of combinations possible—and hence the number of possible different thoughts or brain states each of us can have—exceeds the number of known particles in the entire known universe.[4]

This insight from Dr. Levitin helps put into perspective why we cannot accurately pinpoint how LSD will affect its user from one person to the next. When thinking about the incomprehensible number of connections the brain is capable of making and the way LSD rapidly triggers these connections—and consequently the amount of different "trips" one is capable of having—I tend to think of a never-ending corridor lined with countless doors on either side, each door potentially opening to a limitless number of other doors, each containing the possibility for a different trip. For in my experience, I have found that the slightest variable—a memory, a smell, a song, an accompanying person's vibe, a visual/auditory hallucination, etc.—is capable of completely altering the course of a trip almost instantaneously.

Since there is no exact science of the mind, there is simply no way to predict whether someone will have a *good trip* or a *bad trip*. There is no way to tell whether the user will have mild hallucinations or intense hallucinations, and there is no way of telling what all these hallucinations might consist of. Even within the mind of a person who is well familiar with *tripping*, the spectrum of possibility is so vast that the end result of taking a hallucinogenic substance can be accurately summed up as stepping out into the unknown.

One of the most common misconceptions about LSD along with other hallucinogenic drugs is that they merely produce visual hallucinations. I've met many people who thought these drugs would simply cause you to "see things" while otherwise leaving you in total control of your mental faculties, readily able to separate the hallucination from reality. For instance, the first time I ever *tripped* I had no real way of knowing what to expect, but I imagined it was going to be similar to smoking a joint while also witnessing some of my favorite cartoon characters appear. Nothing could have been further from the truth. The real power of these substances lies in their ability to completely swallow a person's grasp of reality. Oftentimes, the user will become wholly convinced of something that is not at all true, and from there the sights, sounds, feelings, and smells generated serve only to compound and confirm the current psychosis.

To give an example of just how real the thoughts, feelings, and emotions of these experiences can be, let's imagine John Doe getting a call from the United States military, regrettably informing him that his son has been killed in combat. John and his wife process this indescribable grief for a full month, enduring the full spectrum of emotional and psychological challenges that couples face when losing a child. Then thirty days later, they get a call from their son. It turns out the whole thing was one big miscommunication, and he was not actually with his platoon on the day they were attacked.

Now although Mr. and Mrs. Doe have not actually lost their son, they know what it is like to lose a son in every sense of the way. Every day that they crawled forward and struggled to put the pieces together was very real to them. There was nothing staged about their month-long grieving process. Every fit of rage, every suicidal/homicidal thought, every guttural sob they endured was very real.

This same concept applies when it comes to certain experiences hallucinogenic drugs are capable of producing. For example, there is no such thing as 10-foot-tall tarantula. Yet I know exactly what it's like to stare one in all eight of its beady eyes, while simultaneously overcoming a lifetime of arachnophobia. For although these creatures do not actually exist, at the time of its happening, it was as real to me as the ground beneath my feet. In fact, as I stared up at the thing, my exact comment was, "You're not so bad when you're this big, it's just when you're little bitty that you creep me out."

This understanding is vital when it comes to someone who has never had these types of experiences trying to put themselves in the shoes of someone who has.

2

INTO THE RABBIT HOLE

My introduction to psychedelics began the way many dysfunctional relationships begin. The early days were filled with pleasure, enjoyment, and the promise of good things yet to come. Blinded by a false sense of control, I was completely oblivious to what lie ahead.

My first ever *trip* was a journey I took with approximately three and a half grams of psilocybin mushrooms. I was fifteen years old, and never in my entire life had I laughed so hard. In fact, that's all I can remember doing. I was the only one at the small house party I was having who'd eaten the so called "magic mushrooms," and while my other ten or so friends drank their drinks, I slipped off to the computer room in my basement, turned on some music, and laughed uncontrollably for hours. At what exactly? Your guess is as good as mine.

My next couple of *mushroom trips* were equally hilarious, and the hilarity was equally bizarre. Even though I had friends with me who'd also eaten mushrooms on these other occasions, my humor was still a personal brand of random, musical nonsense that led me to a place of isolated laughter. Thus, it was decided and confirmed, I loved mushrooms.

By the time I was sixteen, I was indulging myself in any and every mind-altering substance I could get my hands on. From huffing household chemicals and stealing cold medicine off the shelves of the local pharmacy to furthering my connections in the underground trade, I was like a kid in a candy shop. Up to this point, it was all still fun and games. The closest thing to an overdose or bad trip I'd seen was a friend of mine falling out face first in the midst of filter free laughter after huffing a can of air duster. I guess when I weighed my buddy's few missing teeth against all the good times we were having, play ball it was.

I remember my first ever acid trip was five days before I turned 17, on the Fourth of July. One of my best friends and I dropped two hits apiece, and forty-five minutes later we were off to the races. Again, music seemed to dictate the flow of things, and again the flow of things was extremely comical. I'll spare the details of our adventures, but it's safe to say that after that first time I was sold.

As my teen years transformed into young adulthood, I fell headlong into the music festival and rave scene where my hallucinogenic horizons continued to expand. As I was turning 21, I had dabbled in just about every drug under the sun. I had tripped mushrooms ten or so times, dropped acid twenty or more times, eaten more cold pills than I could begin to count, popped molly and ecstasy whenever present, smoked salvia a couple times, experimented with research chemicals, and had developed a ketamine habit, just to paint the bulk of the picture.

Some trips were intense with vivid, visual hallucinations, while others were defined by indescribable body highs and endless laughs. Sometimes we would go to concerts, sometimes we would throw glow sticks from my deck into the neighbor's pool. Sometimes we'd watch "trippy movies," and one time, I turned the entire sky into a high-def screen that would change channels when I blinked my eyes.

Each trip was its own unique experience. No two acid trips were ever the same, just like no two mushroom trips were ever the same, etc.

Amidst all these great escapes, I had by this time had a couple of bad trips, as well (which I will elaborate on in the chapters to come). Unfortunately, like so many other addicts, I had the uncanny ability to all but totally disregard these horrifying experiences, and in light of all the good times, *keep on rollin'*. It was this cursed ability that would ultimately help pave the way for me writing the rest of this book.

I've written this particular chapter to say, I get it. I understand why we use these substances, and why some would go so far as to champion them as being the key to enlightenment and even being capable of curing mental illnesses. I've been there. I've also been on the opposite and weightier end of the scale too.

3

THE BEGINNING OF THE END

September 2011. How could I have known what awaited me? How could anyone have possibly known? I had recently broken up with my high school sweetheart of five years and as a result was drifting out to some very dangerous waters. We'd had a couple of break ups before, but this time was different, and she wasn't coming back.

I loved her.

At twenty-one, I was a full-blown heroin addict—part of the reason she wasn't coming back. I had developed this habit during the last year of our relationship, and I was pretty good at living a double life while the two of us were together. Once we broke up, though, it all came out.

Living or rather existing at an all-time low, my days consisted of little more than sticking needles in my arm, nodding off while playing video games, and pursuing my next fix. Ashley was my only outlet for affection, and having driven her from my life, I was suffocating. Suicidal depression had taken a vicelike grip on my thoughts, and life was dimming.

It was around this time that one of my best friends was flying back from Northern California. Bucking my reluctance, he was intent on pulling me out of my funk and bringing me back out West, where I'd previously had plans of moving. He showed up to my house around eight or nine at night. I was high. So was he. Only he had been sucking on a bottle of liquid LSD for three straight days. "C'mon, bro," Adam persisted. "You're fine! We're trippin' tonight!"

I had told him I was in a bad place and didn't think acid was a good idea. I should've stood on it. I didn't.

"How much should I do?" I asked, sitting in the backseat of Adam's car. I had tripped acid twenty or so times, but I had never encountered the stuff in liquid form. I would later learn one drop could be equivalent to fifty paper hits.

"Just squirt some on your tongue." Adam responded. Mind you, he hadn't slept in days, and had been at the San Francisco airport for almost two days before he finally figured out how to get on a plane to St. Louis.

I squirted a little drizzle onto my tongue, handed the eye-drop bottle back, and we pulled out of my driveway. We were headed to our third passenger, Dusty's house for the night. Dusty had a finished basement that walked out into an indoor poolroom. It was ideal for tripping.

Before actually making it to Dusty's, the three of us made a few runs, and about thirty minutes after leaving my trailer park, Dusty was asking Adam for some more acid. "Are you sure this stuff's any good?" Dusty asked, "Cuz, I'm not feelin' it."

Adam reassured Dusty that he'd been tripping for three straight days, and I tried reasoning with Dusty that we'd only dosed up a half hour ago, but Dusty persisted, and the end result was all three of us taking another squirt.

By the time we arrived to Dusty's basement, the acid was in full effect. A couple other friends had showed up, and everything was shaping up for a good night.

We had the music going, the weed going, and more people were on their way. One of which was a character I had never seen before.

"Which one of you guys got the acid?" he asked, shortly after showing up.

What happened next blew my mind. After Adam identified himself as the one who would be giving this guy the acid, he asked for it to be dropped in his eye! *No way!* I thought. *That's some 1969 hippy folklore type of stuff!*

After seeing Adam drop a dose in this guy's eye, I had to try it. "Me too." I told him.

"Really?" Adam countered.

"Really."

I share what I'm about to share with you not to glorify the experience, but to further develop the picture of just how deceptive psychedelic drugs can be. For this particular experience would serve as one of the building blocks that would ultimately crumble in my destined collapse.

The effect of the LSD having been administered to my eye was instantaneous. It were as though my brain had received a drink of ice-cold water on a hot summer day. Closing my eyes, I witnessed in perfect clarity my brain light up in an LED, bluish glow, as hairlike strands went from limp and wavy to standing straight up, connecting to the walls of nearby brain matter (whether real or a hallucination, I cannot say). It was in all reality indescribable. As notable as an experience as this was, though, and as much as it stands out in my memory today, it was not long before it was completely forgotten, and I was being swept under by the tide of night.

I remember at some point after the dosing of my eye becoming convinced that the basement was flooded. I felt like I was sloshing around in six inches or so of water, and I found this to be disturbing. It was not just the inconvenience of the water, but the overall vibe had shifted, and I was soon in a place of isolation. As I lost touch with reality, I began to liken the watery situation I was in with the fluidity of time. This led to me conjuring up images of what my parents may have been like when they were my age. The correlation of my parents and their eventual divorce brought Ashley to mind. A very dangerous place for me to be.

By this time, I was oblivious to my surroundings. I'd been taken captive by my thoughts and was becoming untethered to things such as time and space. Amidst my frustrations, I grabbed a glass mug from off the coffee table I was walking past and threw it violently behind me. I did so without breaking stride and without thought of where it might land, almost like a quarterback pitches the ball in an option play, only with greater force. I mention this because I would later learn that the mug hit Dusty in the face and caused some pretty serious damage. Whether or not my friends tried to address this when it happened, I cannot say.

The next thing I remember is laying on the bed in the corner of Dusty's basement, as a multitude of "would you do blank to get Ashley back?" scenarios ran through my head. I would accept each extreme scenario, and a new one would present itself. Then the ultimate scenario presented itself.

For proper context, let's rewind to a couple hours earlier.

Shortly after arriving to Dusty's, we had watched a show that had simulated a battle between a handful of vampires and hordes of zombies. Much to my disbelief, the show gave the victory to the zombies. Being a millennial in the United States, I grew up a fan of vampires, and on this particular night, I became temporarily convinced that I myself was a vampire. As I lay on that bed with scenario after scenario being posed to me, I had the epiphany that I was in fact a vampire, and that in order to reunite with Ashley, I had to slay innumerable zombies to get to her. No problem.

I sat up in the bed and surveyed the basement. *Zombies*. Then my death stare met Adam. This had been one of my best friends since we were thirteen. Could I kill Adam? The war inside my mind was absolute torment. I stared at him in agony, tears welling up in my eyes, trying to process my decision.

I couldn't do it. Adam couldn't be a zombie. *Could he?*

It wasn't long before complete hopelessness set in. My forfeiting to the scenario at hand had sealed my fate. Ashley was gone forever. And with this gripping reality came my decision to end it. Sitting there, light years away from everything aside from my desire to die, I witnessed one of the pistols I owned materialize in my hand. Not only could I see the weapon, I could feel it, as well. The texture, the shape, the weight of it as I jammed the barrel into my mouth. Feeling the barrel press into the back of my throat, I don't remember any hesitation. I squeezed the trigger. Nothing happened. No pain, no bang, no nothin'. I tried again. Still nothing. Infuriated, I cast the faulty weapon aside, named off another pistol I had owned, and watched it materialize just as the first one had. Again, I stuck the barrel in my mouth and squeezed the trigger. Again, nothing. This exercise would go on to include various different guns, as I repeated myself four or five times, growing increasingly frustrated with each failed attempt.

I have been told what happened next was quite freaky to witness. It were as though my physical body were swept up by a whirlwind, as I began spinning around in rapid circles, being thrown back onto the bed. My memories of this event are vague, as my primary focus was locked onto what I began witnessing once on the bed. Differing from the visual hallucinations I had just experienced in my suicide attempts, these images were bright in my mind's eye, much like the vivid clarity of "my brain," I had experienced earlier in the night.

I had entered into some sort of time warp, and the initial scene playing out before me was that of futuristic developments and technological advances. It was like watching a Sci-Fi society from years in the future. This setting played out for a while before shifting to a scene of modern times. I was then in the 60's/70's era. As I drifted further back in time, I began to feel an eerie sense of losing control, and would occasionally state some random fact or opinion, as if doing so were somehow keeping me grounded, preventing me from completely losing it. This continued on for a while, taking me further and further back in time. The further back I went, the faster the film rolled, until I was rapidly passing through ancient landscapes, eventually landing in the "Jurassic Period". I then began to witness the reptiles disappear from off the face of the earth, and all that was left was the planet. It was at this point in the vision that I felt like I myself were the planet. As I witnessed the trees and other plant life retreat into the soil, I felt as though the hairs on my head were retreating back into their follicles. As the mountains broke off into the ocean, I felt my teeth shattering in my mouth. I was watching all of creation vanish, and with this came an overwhelming sense of dread. Everything was ending, and that ending was bad, and I could do nothing to stop it. Terror stricken, I began to cry out random nonsense that I correlated with our current generation, warning what I thought to be the whole world that we "needed to get back to" such things, or else face impending doom.

As earth's foundations collapsed into the ocean, and the ocean swirled into nothingness, I instinctively escaped the tragic ending by opening my eyes.

Dusty's basement. I had survived. We had survived. Phew.

"Dude, are you gonna make it over there?" Adam asked.

"I think we're all going to make it." I responded. "Are you guys smokin'?"

"Yeah, get over here, and quit being so weird."

To be out of my head was strangely foreign, but it was a change I was glad to embrace, nonetheless. Walking over to the ping-pong table where Dusty, Adam, and a couple other buddies were sitting, I remember the music taking hold. In no time I was smiling, laughing, and repeating the hook to the song that was on. Forget the mental anguish of yester year and play that one again! Wow.

I wasn't out of the woods yet, though. As we smoked, joked, and listened to music, another hallucination took center stage. Right in the middle of Dusty's basement an inflatable projection screen manifested itself. The odd thing was I could only see the screen at an angle. What I was seeing, though, was magnificent—a waterfall scene straight from the island of Fiji. That was only the background, though. Credits from the end of a movie were also rolling down the screen. Only these were not just the credits to any old movie, these were the credits to life itself! Hypnotized by what I was experiencing, all else had faded into the distance, and as I watched the credits roll, I was overcome with the sense of having achieved the greatest feat in human history. I couldn't actually read the credits due to the angle of the screen, but I knew they were declaring, "I had done it." I had absolutely no idea what exactly "it" was, but the indescribable feelings were there just the same. *I did it. I really did it.* It was actually so epic, I couldn't bare the idea of taking all the credit.

"Did we really do it?" I asked Dusty. He was the nearest person to me and seemed to be watching the same thing I was. Solemnly, he nodded his head. Now who knows what he really thought I was talking about—he was likely keeping an eye on me, still gun shy from having just been hit in the face with a glass mug earlier in the night—but to me we were on the same page, and his nod was all the affirmation I needed. Again, I began falling into my own thoughts, eyes closed, and isolated from the world around me.

Overwhelmed by these unprecedented emotions, I was soon lost in a world defined primarily by sound. The auditory hallucinations had engulfed my mental state, as I heard cheers, whistles, and the bursting of fireworks. Distinct from the general roar of the crowd, I would hear the familiar voices of different friends and family members saying things like, "Way to go, Scotty!" or "I knew you could do it!"

I still had no idea what it was I had done, just that it was the greatest thing ever. Then the noises of the crowd began to fade into the background, and the most perfect music I had ever heard came into focus. It was some sort of breathtaking, islander, reggae, hip-hop type sound, and the only thing missing was me coming in on the vocals. Next, it became clear that I was on a stage, and on the stage with me were the giggles of various flirtatious women. Finally, taking the foreground was Ashley. I could feel her lips against my ear, as she romantically whispered, "You did it, Scott."

Everything was going to be okay. I cannot describe exactly how I felt in that moment, but as relief and assurance washed over me the sounds of the crowd drifted further off into the distance. "He really did it." "Wow. I can't believe he did it." These somber comments waned to little more than whispers, and then it was over.

I opened my eyes. The message couldn't have been any clearer (as clear as something can be to a mind under the influence of who knows how much LSD). I had witnessed my two possible destinies. I could either continue down the gangster, bad boy, closed emotions, materialistic, heroin addict path I had destructively been on, and die, bringing earth's demise with me, or I could start giving the love I myself so desperately desired, change my ways, save planet earth, and get the girl. This, my friend, was a no brainer.

As day broke, something else very strange was at work. *Why am I still peaking, and why am I so hungry? I must have tapped into something supernatural.* This was all falling in line with the visions I'd had. Or so I thought.

Of all the trips I had previously been on, I should have been coming down. And after a bad experience with a "cheesy gordita crunch" on my third acid trip, rule number near the top while tripping was, no food. But there I was, higher than I'd ever been and starving. "You guys hungry?" I asked, expecting to get a resounding, no. To my surprise however, everyone thought breakfast sounded great, and off we were.

As I walked out of Dusty's basement, I was certain of three things. I had just tapped into the secrets of the universe, I was going to revolutionize the world, and I was going to get Ashley back. Period, period, and period.

CHAPTER THREE PT.2

Fall Out

Hip-hop had played a significant role in my development since around the age of twelve. It became an avenue for me to vent my frustrations, and much like drugs and alcohol, it became a place for me to escape. The more my life gravitated toward criminal behavior, the more the songs I listened to became a part of who I was, as well as who I strived to be. Not only was the music a way of escaping my discomforts, it was motivation, as well.

My infatuation with gangster rap was primarily a relationship of listening. That is until I encountered my first *freestyle cypher* at a party, and inebriated, I joined in. I did this from time to time, and eventually started getting some positive feedback. Like anything else, confidence enhances performance. I was still far too boxed in to ever rap outside of drunkenness, though, and I was too lazy to put time and energy into writing lyrics and creating songs in my alone time. All this was about to change forever.

I had taken the LSD on a Wednesday night, and come Thursday night, I still hadn't slept. Throughout the day on Thursday, my experience was primarily defined by a stimulated mental state, accompanied by intense physical sensations. My hallucinations were confined to my mind's eye, and though bright and vivid in clarity, they were not the sort that completely snatched me away from reason. They were more like seeing really cool stuff with my eyes closed, rather than being swept into some alternate reality where I had no control.

By the time we arrived to the rave that Thursday night, I was in a state unlike any I had ever been in. I immediately began to dance, mingle, and have a time. My social inhibitions had been totally obliterated, and I was consumed with a vibrant embrace toward the world around me. It were as though I had been drinking heavily, only I was clear in my thoughts and physically stable. My logic and belief system may have been severely impaired, but I was nonetheless sharp and cognitive of my surroundings.

Going out back for a smoke, I encountered a couple guys I had partied with once or twice, but other than that didn't know too terribly well. After Wednesday night's "vision," though, just about everyone was my best friend, and we began chopping it up like life-long bros. It was while outback in this smoking section party that somebody kicked off a rap session. This would've been the first time I ever engaged in such a session without being sloppy drunk. It turns out this makes a difference. The lyrics were continuously at my tongue's disposal, and it seemed like I could've gone on for hours. I was for the first time in a long time in my element, and the feeling of such a release, accompanied by the reaction of those in hearing distance determined my future. From that moment on, I began rapping anywhere and everywhere I went.

Friday night came and still no rest. There was a Dub-Step Festival going on that weekend, and as we showed up, my symptoms were near identical to those described in the first paragraph. I was still on my delusional cloud nine, and as I roamed the compound, I was convinced this was going to be the greatest night ever. At some point in the night though, I hit a brick wall. My mind may have been on full throttle zing mode, but my body was on E. I remember finding a friend of mine who had a tent full of air mattresses, and asking if I could borrow one for a while. She agreed, and I carried it along with my blanket and pillow through the crowd and right up to the stage. Front and center. Laying down and pulling my blanket over my head, it wasn't long before the music took hold, and I was a zillion miles removed from everything else around me.

Numerous people tried coaxing me from my little zone, but nothing they were offering was comparing to what I had going on in my own head. I remember the only part of me I would allow out from under the covers was my right arm, which was spazzing to the music like some sort of erratic orchestra conductor. And that's exactly what I believed I was doing—conducting the whole thing with my spasmodic right hand. The music was so perfect the only *logical* conclusion was that I was broadcasting it from my very soul. There was also the little detail that I had signed my name on the consent waiver before entering the festival as, "LSDiesel," and somehow this got back to one of the DJ's, who decided to ad lib, "This is LSDiesel music!" into his mix.

Hook, line, n' sinker.

Having been under my blanket for so long and having completely lost touch with everything but the music, I was soon convinced hundreds of thousands of people had showed up to witness what was happening. The visual, along with the occasional auditory hallucinations taking place in my head were so vivid, I had no need to pop my head out for verification. I can remember as all these people were *showing up*, not only hearing the voice of a well-known rapper offer me a shot of heroin but feeling him take hold of my outstretched arm and inject the needle after I had accepted and feeling the effect as though I had actually intravenously received the drug. I would experience this a couple other times throughout the night with different drugs being pumped into the arm I was conducting with.

Perhaps the crescendo to my hallucinations, though, was being convinced a news helicopter was hovering over me, covering this groundbreaking event. The brightness from the spotlight was blinding, even through my blanket. Over the whirling of the blades,

I could hear the reporter declaring that "god had finally awakened..."

Believing that you are the divine and supreme being of the universe, a being capable of creating and manipulating the elements, naturally leads to many other delusional beliefs, but to me it was all making perfect sense. This was just further confirmation and clarity into Wednesday night's *visions*. This flawed logic immediately became cemented into my personal constitution, and although I had no idea what all it entailed, I left the festival believing I was "god." Having been an atheist for years and thus having a very limited understanding on spiritual beliefs, I had quite the journey ahead of me figuring out *who I was*.

After my experience at the Dub-Step Festival, manipulating my hallucinations became a daily practice. For instance, I would close my eyes, and concentrate until I was able to clearly visualize a favored strand of marijuana. From there, my sense of smell would be tricked into smelling the familiar scent, and I would go through all the motions of rolling and then smoking a blunt that did not exist. I would likewise do this with other intravenous drugs, as well. Another habit became creating fantasy planets in my mind's eye to host concerts on (for the music in my mind was a near constant).

Still yet another trick I became fond of was riding motorcycles and dragons. Of course to the curious onlooker, this committed game of charades must've looked like absolute madness, but to me it was as real as feeling my pet dragon inhale and exhale between my legs as I straddled for takeoff. I was soon convinced if I could think it, I could do it, and if I couldn't witness it happen, I just had to trust it really was...

Amidst all the excitement, I was also battling a severe case of emotional instability. For the first time in my life, I was hearing the voice of my conscience, and in the mirror staring back at me was a monster. Iced arrows from the bow of truth pierced my soul as I thought on the selfishness with which I had treated Ashley. After my *visions*, I had expected everything between us to be fixed, and realizing this was not the case, accompanied by my emotions being thrown all out of whack, left me with a lot of weeping to do when I was not lost in some eyes closed fantasy land.

Come Sunday night, I would get another ate up clue into my newly discovered identity. It was somewhere around two in the morning, and while making a late-night run to the gas station with a couple buddies, I literally spotted *Waldo* (as in *Waldo* from the *Where's Waldo* search and find books). There on the side of the road, with a beanie hat, thick black framed glasses, and a bright red T-shirt with *Waldo's* face taking up the front of it, was the next piece of life's puzzle. I'd found him.

I wasted no time slamming on the brakes and busting a U-turn right there in the middle of the road. Swerving over to the shoulder, I rolled down the window and asked Waldo if he needed a ride. He responded in kind to my child-like invitation, and off we were. To say I was ecstatic would be understatement of the week.

It turns out Waldo was really John, a guy who I had gone to school with. John had fallen on hard times and was at the time living in the woods behind Walmart. Nevertheless, to me he was *Waldo*, and per destiny I had found him.

Once back to my trailer, the four of us smoked some weed, and my other two passengers (Zach and Jared) called it a night. John and I were in it for the long haul, though. I brought him up to speed with everything I had going on, and he played right along. "So do you know who you are?" he asked.

"I think I'm god." I responded, looking for some sort of affirmation.

"Well, kinda. You're the White Lighter." He didn't miss a beat.

"Who's that?" I asked.

"You're earth's guardian angel."

"Really?"

"Yeah. Look in your pocket." Sure enough, I had a white lighter on me. "See. Make sure you keep that on you." he said with an air of mystic wisdom.

The hours flew by as I continued to share my outlandish ideas, and John continued to go right along with them. He also shared some of his own dreams about one day being a famous comedian, and by the time the morning came, I was convinced that not only was he sent to affirm my destiny, but also that he was the funniest person on earth. Surely *the universe* had brought the two of us together.

Monday morning rolled around, and still no sleep (day six out of a total of nine or ten days of sleeplessness). Adam was headed over to pick me up, and *Waldo* declined to spend the day running errands with the two of us. Instead, he was going to head down the street where he knew someone else who lived in my trailer park. I was sorry to see him go but figured his role as a messenger had been fulfilled, and was confident that in due time, I would help him with his comedy career—you know, being *the White Lighter* and all. So I sent him off with a jacket and a survival knife, and never saw him again. I pray he is well.

Adam and I were planning to fly back out to California on Wednesday, but Monday just wouldn't let it be. Our itinerary for the day was pretty loose, and doing my whole *eyes closed thing*, I was content simply being present. By midday however, the two of us were hanging out at a buddy's house who lived in the same neighborhood as Ashley's parents (whom she lived with at the time), and that turned out to be a recipe for disaster.

"Dude, why don't you go talk to Ashley?" This suggestion was thrown out by some wise guy, as I was coming to from a dragon ride.

"You really think she wants to see me?" I countered, in kiddish excitement.

"Of course, she does!" was the resounding consensus from those present. And with that, I was off. Convinced the whole thing was a setup, I thought my buddies and Ashley had been talking, and she was home, just waiting for me to ride in like a knight in shining ripped jeans and white T-shirt.

Should we laugh or cry? It's up to you.

Ashley's house was only about three or four blocks down the street, but as I took off jogging, I imagined I was running some epic cross-country journey. To sweeten the whole deal, I thought the scene was being filmed by *aliens* for the next big Hall Mark commercial. Needless to say, I was pumped. My heart swelled with joy, and making my way down the street, I felt like a king who had just conquered the last of his foes.

She wasn't home. Nobody was. I knocked on the door, and nothing. A bit confused, yet not to be deterred, I went and sat on the curb next to Ashley's mailbox. *Surely, she'll be here any minute.* I thought.

It wasn't long before I had drifted off into one of the concerts in my head. To give you a visual of what this might of looked like, I was sitting there with my eyes closed, arms stretched toward the sky, kind of ebbing and flowing my hands back and forth, in a circular type motion that could be likened unto a mixture of overhead arm circles and hippy dancing. This was "my thing" I did to "braid myself into the universe," allowing for interdimensional travel to far away planets.

I was sitting there, braiding myself into the universe, and shouting out random ad libs when I felt a bright light hit me in the face. I opened my eyes to discover it was a guy across the street, shining a flashlight at me. To my recollection, he didn't say anything, so I went back to doing what I was doing. Nope, nothing to see here.

Then it happened again, and this time it dawned on me, *The light... It's gotta be Ashley!*

I hopped up and walked across the cul-de-sac to investigate. The neighbor was now inside, shining the flashlight from his living room window. No fret. I walked right up on the porch and knocked on the front door. "What do you want?" His tone was stern.

"Is Ashley here?" Mine was warm.

"No. Now get out of here."

"Are you telling me Ashley's not in there watching TV, and you guys are all playing some sort of trick on me?" Still warm.

"No one named Ashley lives here. Now get out of here."

Again, I was a little perplexed by this disappointing exchange, but the shock was short lived, as I walked back over to my concert. It wasn't long before a third light hit me. This one was likened unto the sun, and when I opened my eyes, I did so to the spotlight of a cop car.

The officer called me over and asked if I had any weapons on me and if he could pat me down. I told him I didn't and that he could. After patting me down, we chatted a little bit, and he asked me why my pupils were so big and if I had done any drugs recently. Confusing his friendly demeanor with the fact he was still a cop, I told him I'd dropped some acid a few days ago.

"You don't mind if I go ahead and put you in handcuffs while we talk, do ya?" He emphasized it was just for his safety, and still thinking the whole thing to be some sort of game, I told him that was fine with me. It was right around this time that another officer showed up. He was not nearly as chummy as his coworker, and I remember at some point during his drill down his face morphing into Ashley's. *No way! She's magic too!* I thought, and immediately, I was smiling a ridiculously big smile.

"You think this is funny?" Officer Ashley asked.

"Yupp." I replied, playfully.

"Are we gonna have to do this the hard way?"

"Yupp." Still smiling the nonrefundable smile.

"Put him in the back of the car."

Even as I was being loaded into the back of the cop car, I was unphased. I believed all this was Ashley's way of getting back at me, and soon enough the game would be over, and everything would be happily ever after.

Officer number one and I shot the breeze on the way to the hospital, and he explained they were going to be running some tests on me. He dropped me off, they rolled me in on a wheelchair, and after answering a hundred and one different questions, I was left to myself in the hospital bed. How much time passed before the trickery started, I can't quite say, but it wasn't long before the lady monitoring me started morphing into Ashley, much like officer number two. They all three had blonde hair.

"Ashley..." I whispered, just loud enough for her to hear me.

Finally getting her attention, she just smiled and held her finger to her lips, before looking back to the notes she was taking—*Magical Ashley* playing a practical joke on me, knocking out some homework in the process. "Ashley!" My cracked whispers were now increasing in volume, which got the attention of some of the other nursing staff. They assured me there was no funny business going on and encouraged me to lay back and relax.

A couple minutes later the plot thickened. A nurse showed up to keep me company, and of all the names in all the world her badge could have read, it read, Ashton. A nickname of Ashley's! The lady was about sixty years old and sweet as pie, which left me with only one conclusion—Ashley had traveled back from the future to persist with her tomfoolery. Taking me by the hand, this dear soul did her best to ease my troubled mind. "It's okay, honey. Just lay back, close your eyes, and tell me all about this Ashley."

Holding her hand, I was immediately calmed. I felt great peace knowing that not only was Ashley there, but that she still cared enough about me to do such a thing. I must have held that woman's hand for at least twenty minutes, confessing my undying love, and highlighting all my favorite things about mine and Ashley's relationship. Then it was time for her to go.

The panic was immediate, and instinctively my grip tightened. As soon as she said she had to leave, I became convinced if she left, I would lose her forever. This was yet another test of my love. Would I hold true, or let her slip off into the vastness of eternity? I squeezed that poor woman's hand like a boa constrictor. Soon there were nurses and EMT's everywhere, trying to pry my grip open and pull our hands apart. "I'll never let go! I promise!"

Eventually, however, perspiration did it's part, and the kind old lady's hand slipped from my grasp. Staff members struggled with me from all different angles, eventually lifting me into a stretcher and locking me in wrist restraints. I wasn't fighting in terms of violently throwing blows or seeking to do damage, but I definitely wasn't cooperating either. Finally confined to the gurney, I was rushed to the back of an ambulance where we headed for a hospital with more technology available for running various tests.

Upon arrival to the larger hospital, one of the first things they did was draw blood. "You guys need to take as much as you can get!" I wailed. "My DNA is going to cure the world!" Of this much I was certain.

After a night of delusions, wild hallucinations, and indoctrinating the guy being paid to baby sit me, the morning brought with it a tremendous surprise. My dear mother showed up to the hospital and was going to be sharing a room with me. Somehow, she was contacted, and after receiving some vague details into what all was going on, she rushed to my aid in true momma bear fashion, even bringing with her my childhood blanket. It must have been heartbreaking and terribly disturbing to witness her son in such a psychotic state, but she stayed, and the two of us, along with the babysitters had a grand old time. Thanks, mom.

By the time the following evening rolled around, mom must have been exhausted. Swallowed whole by my psychosis, I spewed forth the contents of my troubled brain with an utter lack of self-consciousness. Granted the shock value of most of this content was comical in nature, some of it was anything but, and my mother was forced to witness her son wrestle through these fits of torment. Not to mention the whole not sleeping thing kept her up into the wee hours of the night, as well.

By the time my third and mom's second night rolled around, I was convinced to leave that particular hospital and go to another. I was told I would not be released, and thus would not be able to smoke a cigarette until I was cleared by the psyche doctors at the other hospital. Remembering certain of my friends had used this other hospital to detox and had received a plethora of pharmaceuticals in the process, I decided this didn't sound like a bad idea. "The sooner the better" instantly became my motto, and an Academy Award winning performance was birthed. I confessed to the heroin addiction, I had previously been denying, and in an instant, went from a wide-eyed boom to the physical lethargy of one suffering from withdrawals and "dope sickness." Correcting my tone of voice, I told the nurses I had been embarrassed, but really, I had been sick the whole time, and that was the real reason for my frequent requests to take a shower. Whether or not they fully bought it or not, within that hour, I was giving my mom a hug goodbye and being wheeled out (I now needed a wheelchair) to the ambulance, headed for the psyche hospital.

The "new" hospital turned out to be the same hospital I was originally admitted to, and we can only imagine their level of enthusiasm at once again having me as a guest. I'm sure they assumed the colorful assortment of high-powered sedatives and psyche drugs would send me the same slumbering way of my predecessors, but to their dismay, I was caught sneaking out of my room a number of times throughout the night to get into the peanut butter cracker cabinet they had previously exposed me to. They were good sports, though, and I was able to avoid the wrist restraints this go around.

I was in need of another Academy Award winning performance if I was to be released from the psychiatric unit. Day after day, I was affirmed crazy by my doctor, and thus I could not pass go. That was until my supporting cast showed up. A friend of mine had arrived a few days into my stay to detox, and the two of us ended up sharing a room together. Seeing how far gone I was and not wanting to see me stuck in the hospital or possibly even transferred to somewhere more permanent, he met me where I was at. "I know what's going on, and you know what's going on, but these people aren't like us, bro." Continuing on, he told me, "If you want to get out of this place, you're going to have to lie to the doctor. Tell her you're back to normal, and you'll be happy to have your dad come pick you up. Tell her you're going to stay with him for a while and get a job. Don't tell her anything about your spaceships or your real plans, or she's not going to sign off on your release." Sticking to the script, I sold my doctor, and after a week in the psyche ward, I was released into my father's custody with a prescription to be filled and a recommendation for inpatient treatment.

CHAPTER THREE PT.3

Still Falling

Once freed from the hospital, life picked up right where it had left off. Many of the people I had known for years were thoroughly entertained by the wild unpredictability I now presented, while others thought it was too much to handle. Even worse, some were altogether frightened. Whatever they thought, it really mattered no never mind to me. I was by and large oblivious to the matters most people think on, and when I wasn't rapping or drifting off with my eyes closed (which was a large percentage of the time for like two straight months, regardless of where I was at or what I was supposed to be doing), I was concocting theories on what lay in store for the human race. Alien revolution was coming, and either you were with it, or you would be when they showed up.

How long the actual LSD ran it's course, I have no way of knowing, but at some point, during my stay in the psyche ward, I did begin to sleep for a couple hours here and there. This sleep seemed to mesh an immediate dream state into the hallucinations of my mind's eye, one picking up where the other left off. I seemed to be semi-conscious of what was happening even as I slept. As the weeks or perhaps months went by (again I have no exact way of knowing), and the drug itself began to where off, the aftermath was a condition doctors have labeled, "Persistent Psychosis." I have another belief on this particular diagnosis, which I won't elaborate on, but ultimately it were as though I never stopped "tripping." The hearing of voices, along with visual disturbances and the rewiring of my overall belief system were residual effects I dealt with for nearly two years. If I were to exhaust every hallucination and unusual story from this period, you would be holding a multi volume encyclopedia, so I'll stick to the scenes pertinent to our book's purpose.

A few weeks after being released from the hospital, I was staying at a friend's house, when a door-to-door salesman showed up. I can't recall what the guy was selling, but I'll never forget what transpired while talking to him. The two of us were joking on my buddy's front porch, when he turned pitch black before my very eyes. From head to foot, he was a total abyss in human form, and without hesitation, I addressed him as being the devil. Surely if I were god, it wouldn't be strange for the devil to show up. "Really?" I interrupted. "You're going to show up at my friend's house?" Turning on a dime, I went from fun and games to *dead serious*. When you grow up with Batman as your hero, and then you have that type of vigilante complex amplified to eternal proportions, things can get dangerous quick.

I can't recall the salesman's exact response, but I know I followed by giving him the ultimate ultimatum. "If you don't get out of here right now, I'm going to kill you." Thank God, this guy took me at face value. Apologizing for any confusion, he hurried back to his car.

Over the next couple months, I bounced around between my friend's house, my dad's house, and one of the local motels, before my mom seized her opportunity to get me to come and live with her. It was Thanksgiving weekend, and she invited to come stay for a few days. Thinking this to be a *sign from the universe*, I took her up on her offer, and off I was.

Along with my stepdad, stepbrother, and two little sisters, my mom had just recently moved back to Missouri, herself, from Virginia, where the four of them had been living for the past three years. Actually, at the time of my arrival, they were still in the process of finishing building a house on the property my mother had inherited, at the passing of my grandfather (a six-acre plot, which is sectioned off from a significantly larger piece of land that is divided up amongst various other family members in beautiful, rural Missouri). Everything just seemed to have the vibe of *coming together*. I had known these woods since the time of my birth, and along with rekindling relationships with my family, being back in the old familiar scene, away from the hustle and bustle of society, had a definite impact on my growth. The stillness of the country and the serene beauty that came with it was quite refreshing after my many years of superficial monotony.

A series of unfortunate events, combined with long distanced living, had taken a toll on my relationship with my family, and reconnecting with them was a far greater joy than I had originally anticipated. I had grown so cold and selfish over the years, I had totally lost sight of what it was to truly love. I was changing, though. I was different, and although this different may not have been clinically stable, it was a different that allowed me to love much more freely than I or my family had previously known.

About a quarter mile down the old, rock road from my mom and stepdad's house is my aunt and uncle's place. Well, it just so happens that right as I was making my own move to the family property, my cousin, Rodney was doing the same. Having just broken up with his fiancé, back to mom and dad's it was. No doubt, this played a major role in me deciding to stay for more than just the weekend. The two of us had always been close, but the bond we would forge during this particular season of life was beyond what either one of us could have expected.

Rodney had been a thinker for as long as I could remember and had been delving into the realm of abstract theories for quite some time before I came along. This made him as interested in what all I had going on as anyone, and with the prospect of this curious spectacle now before him, he was just as eager to share as I was to learn. Combined with some of my own outlandish input the two of us made quite the pair. A couple of wandering souls, combing through YouTube videos for life's answers. And when we weren't doing that, we were likely out at the bars, where I was giving hugs and preaching revolution, and he was enjoying having me around.

"I think you might be the craziest person on earth... And I think there should be some sort of award for that." Ever my biggest cheerleader, my mother's words were both lighthearted and sincere at the same time.

"Oh, mom..." I chuckled, placing my hand on her shoulder. I really did pity those who thought I was crazy, because that meant they were missing out on *enlightenment!*

Armed with little more than a genuine desire to pump love into a world full of hurt and an unwavering belief that destiny had ordained such a thing; I was on a mission. My overall perception may have been delusional at best, but the hallucinations in my mind's eye were subsiding, and my cognitive thinking was gradually returning, which allowed for more effective communication with the world around me. Once a stranger to the little college town of Rolla, Missouri, I soon knew and was known by more people than I could count. After wearing out my last pair of contacts (without which I am legally blind), I took it as a *sign from the universe* that I was to rely more heavily on the supernatural for guidance. The result of which was, a lot of times, me greeting just about every last person at whatever party or bar I was at. After a couple incidences where people I had formed epic bonds with just the night before came up to me and said, "Dude! What's up?! You didn't see me over here, or what?" I started taking the proactive approach. Certainly revolution would never take off if its leader couldn't even recognize his own friends! And thus, the logical solution was to begin greeting anybody and everybody, sharing my bright ideas with whoever was willing to entertain me.

Growing up with an extended family where affection was often conveyed via hugs, I decided if I was gonna get this planet turned right side up, hugs would be a good place to start. Naturally, however, not everyone understood the innocence of the gesture, and thus a game plan had to be formulated. Let's use "John" and "Jenny" as an example. John is kind of a tough guy, Jenny is a pretty college girl, and John is leery my whole hippy revolution rhetoric just might be laced with ulterior motives. No problemo. "I dig it. I dig it. You're too cool for hugs. What about rhymes? You guys like rhymes?" Here's a better question, who doesn't like rhymes? Hence, I was never told, no. The "yeah" may have come out with a hint of confusion, sounding more like a question than a statement, but I never got a "no, I don't like rhymes."

"Awesome," I would reply. "I love rhymes. John, what type of work do you do?"

"Umm, I'm a full-time student. Why?"

"Just bear with me. What about you?" Now directing my question toward Jenny.

"I work at Tina's Pizzeria."

Maybe I'd ask a couple more generic questions, maybe not, but once equipped with this information, I would break out a customized freestyle. Deal sealer. Whatever reservation had previously existed was annihilated by the personalized rap, and in the midst of their shock and excitement, the hugs came automatically. "Huh, see?" I would laugh, "I knew you guys were huggers!"

From there, the atmosphere was ripe for nonsensical jargon about earth's soon coming transformation—a glow in the dark planet, fully capable of morphing surface textures to suit the changing desires of her inhabitants, while at the same time producing incomprehensible music, also predicated on the preference of the listeners in that particular vicinity. John would soon learn the only interest I had in Jenny was the same interest I had in him, and that was that the both of them would drop society's chains and pick up the *revolution*. Near identical scenes played out who knows how many times.

Surely, I was lost as a ball in high weeds, but this was my life. I hung out with my family. I rap battled myself in the woods outback, sometimes getting four or five different voices in on the action. I scoured YouTube with my cousin and dear friend, Rodney. I gave watches, hats, necklaces, and jackets away at gas stations to complete strangers, responding to their bewilderment with, "I just wanted to say, thanks for being on planet earth with me." I got kicked out of all kinds of places, while getting preferential treatment at others. From Thanksgiving of 2011 to April 18, 2012, I bounced from couch to couch, in rural Missouri, preaching grandiose nonsense everywhere I went.

I met a lot of people along the way, and to any reading this who I may have negatively influenced, I sincerely apologize.

In my original writing of *LSDerailed*, I refrained from elaborating on my belief as it pertains to the clinical diagnosis of "Persistent Psychosis," but as will be made perfectly clear throughout the extended chapters, I believe this diagnosis equates to satanic possession. I believe I had been possessed, and the voices I was hearing were those of devils. I believe schizophrenia (a symptom of Persistent Psychosis) is likewise evidence of possession. The root to this mental torment is spiritual depravity, and those suffering from this type of satanic attack do not need pills, they need the anointing power of the Holy Ghost. Only the anointing will do.

4

MY APOCALYPSE

We all have moments in life where the outcomes are irreversible. We've all made decisions that birthed consequences we simply couldn't undo, and as a result, have had to face the devastating reality we have created. For me, perhaps this truth has been most defined by the night of April 18, 2012.

It was a weeknight, middle of the week. I had a probation meeting the following day, and my stepbrother, Eli had a flight to Boston scheduled for that same morning. Both our appointments were in the St. Louis area, and instead of waking up at the crack of dawn to make time, we decided to drive up that night and stay the night at my dad's. With Eli's car not having plates, and me not having a car, contacts, or sanity, we caught a ride with Jessica, a friend of the family.

Jessica happened to have some LSD.

Convinced acid was the *key to enlightenment*, I had zero reservations about dosing up the night before going in to see my probation officer. Jessica and Eli had never tripped before, and I was just excited for them to hopefully have some epiphanies of their own. Whether it was my continual and charismatic promotion of the drug or simply their own individual curiosity, I'm not sure, but the three of us decided dropping acid was a good idea for the night, even when most would have thought the timing to be less than rational.

Pulling into my father's trailer park, the acid was climbing toward its peak. We sat out in the driveway, and smoked a blunt, after which I suggested a nature hike. It was absolutely beautiful outside, and not ten minutes away were some bike trails leading to a nearby conservation area. Eli thought the woods sounded worthwhile, but Jessica sided with staying in her van and watching *trippy* videos of swirling colors and such on her iPhone.

Forty-five minutes or so into our adventure, Eli got a text from Jessica, saying she was cold, and wanted to go inside. Once inside, the three of us plopped down on the sectional that took up the better part of my dad's living room. Trying to create an acid friendly environment, I flipped through the music channels on the TV and decided on reggae. From there, we all huddled around Jessica's phone to watch the trippy swirling color videos. Then, at some point, Jessica got up to go to the bathroom, and losing the entertainment of the iPhone, I was soon nestled deep in the crevices of my own thoughts.

For eight straight months, I had grown more and more convinced by the day that it was my burden to bring about universal peace. I had yet to pinpoint exactly how I was supposed to accomplish this, and thus I was constantly searching for answers and solutions. I was open to just about anything, and anything was fast approaching the point of no return.

Reincarnation had long been a staple to my ever-developing theories, and on this particular night the story playing out in my mind went something like this:

Jessica was in the bathroom crying of a broken heart. Why? Because billions of years ago her and her soulmate had been mercilessly ripped apart from each other. As Earth's first woman, she had shared a perfect love with Earth's first ever man. Somehow, though, disaster struck, and the two were torn apart, destined to one day reunite. I was Earth's first ever man.

Throughout the eons the two of us had reincarnated at various times, but never at the same time or in the same place, our souls ever seeking one another. Well, after all the countless generations, here we were, and she was conscious of the fact. She was conscious, and she was broken hearted that I no longer loved her.

All this time, this was the answer I had been searching for. All the world needed was original love to once again blossom. The universe had finally aligned the lock and key to the whole thing, and yet I was too shallow to even consider it.

The gravity of the situation was suffocating me. I felt like my thoughts were exposed to all creation. It were as though my mind was a reality TV show, and the entire universe was watching in anticipation for me to *save the day*. Every second I delayed, I became ever more the monster. The civil wars in Africa, the sickening poverty in Calcutta India, the broken homes littering the United States, the grotesque abuse of children all over the globe, every tear that fell, and every shout of rage that echoed in the ears of its recipient... I could hear their cries, and yet I was frozen from action. It was all being prolonged by the shallow rise and fall of my own chest.

With tears in my eyes and a hurricane in my heart, I looked to Eli, "Is this real?" I asked, positive that he knew exactly what was going on. Much like the scene in Dusty's basement, he gave me a nod, and that was all I needed. I rushed to the bathroom at the end of the narrow hallway and knocked on the door. "Jessica, are you decent?"

She opened the door almost immediately, and I remember my first thought being that she had been "stuck" in the mirror (a common misfortune that plagues first time trippers when they find themselves overwhelmed by the distorted image staring back at them). She had been in the bathroom awhile, and when she opened the door, she was facing toward the sink with her eyes wide as they could get. Never mind the mirror, though, I was on a mission. "Jessica," I blurted out, "Marry me!"

Only when the words left my mouth, no great cosmic shift occurred, and I immediately regretted what I had just said. The weight of the world was replaced by the blaring truth that I had zero feelings for this woman, aside from platonic. I failed to confess to my mistake right away, but after a bit of awkward back and forth, I hurried back to the living room in a "wait, what just happened?" type dash.

By the time Jessica made it back to the living room, I was sitting cross legged on the floor, next to the ottoman near Eli, who was still on the couch. Jessica sat down on the opposite end of the couch, and almost immediately, I confessed to not being able to marry her. What a relief! Only it wasn't. I may have gotten that off my chest, but more was piling on. With only the faint glow of the TV, an uncomfortable silence washed over the darkened room, and I was once again wandering the caverns of paranoia.

How the sharing of the cigarette came about, I can't recall. Perhaps Eli saw that I had gotten lost, and was a million miles away, and was trying to bring me back. I can't really say, but by the time the last drag had been taken, the battle had been lost. As my younger brother went to stand up, I leapt from my seated position and met him across the face with the thick glass ashtray that had been sitting next to him on the ottoman. As he fell back into the couch, I straddled on top of him and continued the assault until my father came racing across the kitchen in shouts of distress.

In the five minutes or so it takes to smoke an Edgefield 100, here's how the chips had fallen: Eli was not really my stepbrother. He was a world renown assassin. Upon close observation, this much was certain. He had been tormenting and oppressing my family in the most volatile of ways, only they hadn't told me out of fear for their lives. The voices were back, and so was the weight of the world. Everybody was watching, waiting, on the edge of their seats. Completely helpless to recognize the fact I had just encountered near identical emotions only to find out they were born of delusion, I had once again arrived at the pinnacle ultimatum. Would I walk in faith, avenge my own flesh and blood, seize my destiny, and usher in utopia, or would I cower down in front of all creation, have my head blown off, and spend eternity in some desolate wet ditch while people walked by spitting on me, urinating on me, throwing trash on me, and saying things like, "Yeah, there's Scotty. Straight lame. He had the chance to save us all but was too scared to even stick up for his own family. Now we're stuck living like this for another billion years."

The crescendo of it all was unbearable. I could hear the voices of onlookers far and wide. I could feel their eyes boring into the back of my skull. The *aliens*—the fallen—were loud and persistent as ever, encouraging, threatening, coaching, demanding. I could hear the brokenness and see the tears of those I loved the most. I could hear my father arguing with a group of men who were badmouthing me, wagering everything he owned that I would prevail and avenge the family name. I could hear Eli admitting to guilt and owning up to what was about to happen to him if I chose to *wake up*, while at the same time assuring me that if I failed to act, he was going to go out to Jessica's van, grab the pistol, and execute me.

As this whole scenario is building, Jessica asks Eli to run out to her van, and grab her *phone charger*—code for the pistol. My suspicion was confirmed when I offered to go grab the charger, and Eli assured me that it was no big deal and that he would get it. Why didn't I just go out to the van anyway? Because my good old alien buddies had responded with, "Beasts don't use pistols. You're an animal, and tonight you'll finally awaken to that." This seemed to make perfect sense, and so I remained seated. I remained seated in absolute torment, trying to no avail to occupy my thoughts with that nasty little cigarette.

And then it happened again! "Eli, will you please go get my charger?" Once again, I offered my services and once again, I was met with an identical response. I was now certain I was being toyed with. Eli knew that I knew, but on the surface nobody could say anything. I had to act in faith in order for everything to be properly accomplished. It were as if Eli was saying, "You don't get it yet? You're not allowed to get the gun. You've gotta play by the rules, and if you don't do something soon, best believe I will."

As if all this weren't enough, the lyrics playing from the TV had suddenly come into focus, "You're blinded by angels..." At the time, the true depth of these words went right over my head, and I interpreted them as, *Are you kidding me? Have I been so blinded by this whole hippy dippy, one love, peace crusade that I'm just going to sit here with the person who's committed these atrocities, and not do anything about it? Have I completely lost all sense of who I am?* On top of all the other emotions that had been bubbling over, I was now consumed with rage.

The cigarette was coming to an end. My blood had started to boil. The voices were so loud I couldn't stand it. Eli was moving to get up. Act or get acted on.

"What's going on?!" my dad shouted, as he stormed out of his back bedroom, across the kitchen, and into the living room. This scared me half to death and sent me into an even greater state of confusion. Without hesitation, I hopped off Eli and began pleading my case.

I don't know how long this particular scene lasted, but from what I've gathered it wasn't long before I resorted back to paranoia driven violence. Mom tells me we were on the phone, but only for a minute when it went dead on my end. Dad says I was standing on the front porch, smoking a cigarette, staring off a million miles into the distance when I dropped the phone from my ear. I can't recall. What I do remember is my dad gently taking my face in his hands, and trying to assure me that he loved me and that everything was going to be okay. I likewise remember this sending me into another episode. This was not the nature of mine and my father's relationship, and his intentions were instantly thought to be false. Whatever I had been thinking before, I was now hit with accusations toward my own father. The list of horrors had compounded, and he was in on it.

Our next available memory takes us to the back bedroom, opposite end of my father's. My one-time bedroom, these four walls quickly became instruments of torture, and what lasted only minutes seemed like an eternity. I could stand the scattered pacing no more. I had to get out of there, and when I did so, I emerged convinced my life was one big conspiracy. Everyday people, people who smiled at me, sold me groceries, known me since my youth, they were nothing more than veneers. They knew who I was—the universe's right hand of vengeance—and had been doing everything in their power to keep me from waking up. For though they masqueraded in my presence, behind my back they committed gruesome crimes of the most hideous sort. Only tonight there would be no more hiding. I was awake, and before nirvana, there would be war. One night only. Eradication.

The best I can liken my reality to as I exited my one-time bedroom was like the last level of a violent video game. Enemies were going to be crawling out of the woodwork, coming in from all different angles. The voices in my head had hyped me up beyond the confines of fear-stricken paranoia, and into a very dangerous realm of pride. I was ready for justice, and justice demanded combat. So as I entered the hallway, I did so with a medieval mace in my right hand (for those unfamiliar with such a weapon, it was a baseball bat like club, around two feet in length, with two-inch spikes protruding from the upper quadrant of it).

My father met me in the middle of the hallway, and I can only imagine what washed over him when he saw what I was holding. "Are you going to hit your own father with that thing?" he asked, after attempting to take the weapon from me, which I yanked away, and raised for a blow. I told him, I would. I told him, I would kill him and that I didn't trust anyone. Grasping at straws, I told him, if he really loved me, if he was really on my side, he needed to leave. Because anything else I was going to take as an attack on my life. Try as I might, I cannot for the life of me picture the look on my father's face or how he responded to my desperate plea for him to leave.

The spirit of war I had exited my room in was melting away, and once again, I was gripped with fear and uncertainty. I didn't want to kill my dad. I loved my dad. But at the same time, was he really my dad? I just wanted him to leave. I wanted everyone to leave. Not everyone did, though.

Once again, retreating to my bedroom, a near identical scene began playing out. I was extremely hot and feeling extremely trapped. I felt ridiculous, like some sort of caged animal who was disgracing his very purpose for being. Once again, I was overwhelmed with rage, and a thirst for war was overriding all other thoughts and emotions. I didn't know what all to expect as I exited my bedroom for the last time, but I knew I couldn't stay a second longer.

Entering the living room, I found Jessica sitting on the couch. My dad and Eli had left, she had not. The moment I laid eyes on her, it became perfectly clear that she was the one who had murdered my cousin, Annie (who had been shot just four months prior). She had taken her life to take her place, and her attempts at helping to solve Annie's case had been mere charades to get in good with my family. Not only had she perpetrated this crime against my own family, though. Her criminality was serial in nature, and she had executed this same exact blueprint in homes all across the country.

Having already been consumed by a spirit of hostility, I didn't wrestle with this delusional scenario near as long as I had with the others. The details developed rapidly, and I believed them. My only contention was an engrained belief, since childhood, that it was wrong for men to hit women. This brief flare of hope, however, was immediately snuffed out upon hearing, "Tonight's the night that all get's set back in order, Scotty. There's going to be a lot of bloodshed tonight, and we love you enough to have first given you the woman who killed your cousin, in cold blood. It ends tonight, and it starts with her." All else had vanished. Ten minutes ago, ten years ago— nothing outside of that very moment existed.

As if on cue, the speakers in my head came to life—a heavy beat with an intro consisting primarily of dark and eerie pipe organs. In the background, were the sounds of live warfare—machine gun bursts, the chopping of helicopter blades, civilians screaming... And echoing through it all was an old familiar ad lib, "Flocka!" *The universe had spoken.*

In the extreme violence that would ensue, I can only attribute what took place to Divine Intervention. After already having been assaulted to the floor, in her panic and terror, Jessica began frantically crying out on the name of Jesus. I'll never forget that. And when I went to strike her again, the club snapped clean in two, sending me into a state of confusion and giving her the opportunity to escape.

As it is with a paper towel sopping up a spill, so it was with the rose, on my arm. Upon the club breaking, I fell to my knees in utter confusion. *My chosen weapon, broken? How can it be?* I held out my hands searching for answers, and as I did so, my eyes locked onto the tattoo covering my right forearm—a black rose. A small droplet of blood had appeared on one of the petals, and as I stared, it gradually increased in size, just like a paper towel sopping up a splash of cranberry juice. Soon the entire flower was soaked, and blood was beginning to run down my arm. It was then that a light of potential clarity tried clicking. *Am I trippin'?* I thought. *Did I almost just kill Jessica, and I'm trippin'?* I needed to get to my mom and sisters. They'd have the answers.

On impulse, I jumped up and headed for my neighbor's house. Surely, he'd lend me his car for the night. Here's the thing, though, aside from the fact I was about to show up unannounced at two in the morning to see if I could borrow his Suburban, I was also completely naked. Why was I naked? At some point before my attack, I had become disgusted with the fact I was wearing clothes. I took it as a direct insult to my primal nature. *What do they think, I'm some kind of circus monkey?* For months, I'd believed that humanity should get back to a more "natural" way of living, and on April 18, I took a stand for it. I was an animal, and never again would I be mocked with articles of clothing.

Before making it to the trailer across the street, I encountered Jessica's minivan. I was immediately flooded with frustration. What was I supposed to do? Should I fall to my knees and desperately apologize, or should I finish bringing justice to a serial killer who had murdered the girl that had been like a sister to me my entire life? I didn't know. Irritated, I hit the driver's side window, as I walked past. Not a fully cocked blow with the intent of damage, but a frustrated jab as I walked by.

I never made it across the street. My dad had called the police.

I didn't receive this man as someone who could help me, nor did I receive him as an officer of the law. I took him as a threat to my wellbeing and evidence that war had in fact kicked off. His shouting commands and pointing weapons were confirmation that enemies of all sorts would soon be coming in from the North, East, South, and West. My innate, fight or flight response kicked in, and unfortunately, I chose to fight.

The officer was on the ground with me on top of him before it ever registered, he might not in fact be the enemy. I was choking him from behind when I consciously noticed the flashing lights for the first time. Then, taking note of the man whose neck was tightly secured in my arm, the fact that he was in uniform began to register. It was in this moment that another wave of clarity tried breaking through. *Is this a cop? Scotty, are you choking a cop right now?* A sobering fear began to take hold but was just as soon snuffed out by another *sign from the universe*. A group of late-night teenagers just so happened to be walking down the street, and the sight of me on top of the officer brought about drunken cheers for me to continue the assault. Having heard from the *powers that be*, I released the choke hold and began to land repeated blows with my right fist. Before losing consciousness, the officer reached his service weapon over his shoulder and squeezed the trigger.

"Get down!" "Lay down!" "Get down!" My next memory is that of being surrounded by officers, all shouting and pointing guns. Perhaps they weren't all yelling, perhaps they weren't all pointing guns, but enough of them were that I felt as though an entire military company had surrounded me. I was on all fours, trying with everything in me to stand up, when I noticed the gaping holes in my chest and left forearm. How on earth my heart was still beating seemed a bit of a mystery, but I was certain the chunk missing from my arm was a zombie's doing. The trajectory of the bullet had hit my arm in such a way that the flesh on the outside bend of my elbow had been laid completely open, exposing both meat and bone alike. *A zombie bite*. Not only were the men surrounding me the most diabolical breed of criminals, but they were also zombies. I had to get up.

"God! If I am who you say I am, give me strength to defeat them!" Gasping between syllables, this cry was a follow up to having the effects of a Taser cycle through my body. After my futile plea, I gathered up the last of my energy and made one final surge to stand. My attempt was met with more electricity, and this time I collapsed to the ground. Finally subdued, the officers cuffed me and hoisted me onto a stretcher.

My last memory of the night is from the back of the ambulance. As the paramedics sped off, I was strapped to the gurney, thinking, *They're going to break my neck. That's how they're going to do it.* As the driver punched down on the accelerator, I thought his intent was to gain enough speed, that when he slammed on the breaks, I would be sent rolling forward at such a rate that my spine would snap on impact. Since the wound to the chest and the infected saliva hadn't done the trick, this would be their next attempt.

When I woke up, I was cuffed to a hospital bed.

Though causing four holes, only two shots were fired. The "zombie bite" ended up lodged in my sternum, bruising the lining of my left lung. It had passed clean through the outside of my left forearm, exiting my bicep and entering into my left pectoral. Allegedly, the second bullet came after the first had gotten me off the officer's back, but I pursued again in my attack (I can neither verify, nor deny, as my memory blacked out after the first shot was fired). This bullet nearly blew out my femoral artery as it hit my right thigh about seven or eight inches down from my waist. Had either one of these 40 caliber bullets hit a hair this way or that, the doctor said they would have likely proven to be fatal.

Although I, along with everyone else had survived this treacherous night the terror was far from over.

Though bearing resemblance to the events that transpired, the officer's testimony of the incident was full of errors. It is my belief, he had to justify why things went the way they did, and I will always believe that had he approached this volatile scene differently and obeyed his directive to stand by and wait for back up, our conflict could of been avoided all together. This being said, once having made the decision to engage me, I believe the officer reacted appropriately, and my sincerest of sympathy goes out to him and his family.

Refraining from preaching in the first edition, I must now shout praises unto the Most High God! To see the mighty hand of Jesus on display at the very mention of His glorious name is not something to be taken lightly. And to anyone reading this who may yet be skeptical of God's supernatural working in lives of people, here in the twenty-first century, doubt no more! Surely, the Lord Jesus Christ is the same yesterday, today, and forever. He is the LORD who changes not, and His power is as sovereign today as it has ever been, and by the grace of God, ever shall be. Amen, and in Jesus' mighty name, Amen!

5

REAPING THE WHIRLWIND

My dramatic exit from society was the result of never having fortified my position in the battle for my mind. From the earliest of my teen years, I had sought to escape rather than to fight. As a coward does on the front line, I ran from my struggles, retreating into the abyss of substance abuse. I never dug deep and developed a character capable of standing in the heat of battle. The consequence being, when my sanity began to slip, I had no tethers to secure me from floating off into strange and ominous territories. I had spent my life sowing seeds, with absolutely no understanding of what my harvest might one day look like.

My stay in the hospital was no less torturous than my time spent in my bedroom the night before. The police were not allowing anyone to see me, and the four or five days I spent in isolation chained to that bed were maddening. Aside from the voices in my head, the TV and the radio were talking to me, as well. Every channel and every station seemed to be communicating to me in very undesirable ways. To give one brief example: While trying to find a moment of solace in the oldies station, I keyed in on the lyrics, "Midnight Train From Georgia". The message was clear. A well-known rapper from the south had heard that I could beat him in a rap battle and was headed my way on a "midnight train". Chained to the hospital bed, I was soon to experience the twisted wrath of this particular artist. Surgical saws, scalpels, medical scissors, etc. He was on his way.

After enduring multiple like scenarios, I was eventually taken to the County Jail, where the torment would finally subside. Due to my injuries, along with my unpredictable behavior, I was held in an area of the jail isolated from the rest of general population. I was placed in a cell by myself, where I was able to make my first phone call since having been arrested. "Mom!" I cried, as my mother picked up on the other end of the line. "I don't know which voices to listen to! I just want it to stop!"

"You listen to me, Scotty. You don't listen to any of those voices! I love you. We all love you. It's going to be okay. Just remember the love. Remember what you were trying to find before all this happened." My mother was firm, while yet full of tender compassion, and the relief I felt at finally hearing her voice cannot be articulated in finite words. Her loving affirmation brought an immediate peace, and for the first time since coming to from my chemically induced coma in the hospital, I was able to rest. The onslaught of violent scenarios and the deafening voices that accompanied them had vanished.

The court room where I was called to be arraigned of my charges seemed more like a prop to a play than a legitimate setting where people's lives hung in the balance. I don't know what exactly I was expecting, but I just remember the whole scene being very surreal. Artificial and cheap as things may have seemed at first, it all got real, real quick, when the judge opened his mouth and started talking. The sickening turn of my stomach at hearing I was facing the rest of my natural born life behind bars was not at all what I had anticipated. It was like getting sucker punched—like getting the unexpected news that your parents were getting divorced or that your best friend had just been killed. You can't believe it, much less actually process it, but no matter your ability, the die has been cast, and there's nothing you can do to bring back what once was. My bond was set at half a million dollars, and as it stood, I was facing life in prison.

After about a week, the guards determined I was no longer as volatile of a threat, and I was moved from my place of isolation to a pod designated for men with violent crimes. Much like the cell I had been staying in, the cells in H-Pod were also designed for one man rather than two—a dynamic that would prove to be invaluable. Not only was I sober for the first time since being a young teen, but I was also free from the distractions of society for the first time ever. I had long deprived myself of quality, clear-headed alone time, and what I would discover in the months to come surpassed anything I had previously dreamt possible.

Crazy as a loon, I may have still been, but at least I was back to a "thank you for being on planet earth with me" type of crazy. Much like my mom had suggested, I went right back to where I was before getting arrested. Though delusional, I believe this helped me cope with the severity of my situation. I thought it was all part of the plan and didn't allow my mind to overwhelm itself with thoughts of what my outcome would be. Love, peace, and revolution —that was the outcome.

My unique demeanor also paved the way for me to establish some pretty deep relationships with the guys I lived with. Aside from a few minor altercations, I got along great with everybody, and our pod of twenty-four actually had sort of a family vibe to it. I even began ending every night, after we all got locked down, by going to my door and kicking a closing rap for everyone. Whether or not every last person enjoyed this, I never heard any different.

When I wasn't hanging out in the day room or playing basketball, I was in my cell. It was more like a sanctuary to me than it was a place of punishment. I was further discovering who I was created to be, and the fascination and the depth of such a journey superseded any oppression the place may have offered. I kept strange hours, staying up until breakfast and then sleeping until dinner, having the nights all to myself. Along with rediscovering my childhood love for reading, I discovered a previously unknown passion for writing. I wrote poems, songs, letters, books, and took notes, whenever I felt I had a worthwhile idea. And when I wasn't reading or writing, I was listening to music, thinking, or working out. Truly, I would not exchange this experience for ten million worlds.

One of the hardest things I've ever done was tell Ashley, I wasn't in love with her anymore. This was not really the case, but I felt like it was what I had to do. Well, let's rewind just a little bit.

After moving to Rolla, Ashley and I had started mending our relationship. She was actually contemplating switching schools at the end of the semester and moving down there with me. Then April 18th happened.

With the amount of time I was facing, I made the executive decision that running Ashley off was best for both of us. Perhaps this was wrong. Perhaps I should have given her time and supported whatever she decided. I assumed her decision for her, though, and thought I would save us both a lot of pain and heartache by making the cut as clean and immediate as possible. I wrote her a letter, telling her how much I appreciated her and how I would always love her, but I just wasn't "in love with her" anymore. I told her that even if I got out that very day, we just weren't meant to be. At the time nothing could have been further from the truth, but in desperation and immaturity I did what I thought had to be done.

About a year into my stay and just shy of my twenty-third birthday, things began breaking off into the sea. For the duration of my psychosis, one of my beliefs had been that I was destined to break the law of physics. I believed I could ascend to a state of being able to fly, walk through walls, and morph my physical appearance, just to name a few. After dedicating nearly two years of my life trying to figure this whole thing out, though, my patience was wearing thin. I was either going to ascend or die trying. I told my mom over the phone that I loved her, and if I died, not to worry, we'd meet again. I informed her that I was going to be going to the hole where I was going to isolate myself from all human contact, strip down to my bare humanity, and go without food or water until I either died or achieved my destiny.

Now the book in your hands testifies to my wellbeing, and yet you also never caught the breaking news story about Superman's world debut, so what happened? After the phone call with my mom, a very strange and powerful string of events began taking place, which ultimately culminated in me finding what I had so desperately been searching for. God.

Not only did this encounter save my life, but it also brought about the restoration of my sanity. A mind that was for all practical purposes broken received instantaneous healing. It was an experience unlike anything I had ever tasted of, and from that moment on, I was different. I guess I was *different* before I was different, but this was a much better different. Just ask my mom.

Come September, we were going to trial. The prosecutor's "plea bargain" of twenty years in prison didn't seem like much of a bargain, and so my family helped to get me an attorney. The understanding was that we would be presenting a "Diminished Capacity" defense, which would have contended that on the night of my arrest, I was not mentally competent enough to comprehend and logically think through the consequences of my actions. I was more than willing to admit to my guilt, just not under the pretense of it having been some coldblooded, calculated act of random violence.

I'll spare you chapters worth of legal jargon and courtroom theatrics, but suffice it to say, I lost. My attorney did not in fact present the defense we had discussed, nor was any of the key evidence regarding my mental health history brought forth for my jury to see. I don't believe my attorney *threw the game*, so to speak, there just happened to be a significant misunderstanding somewhere along the way. The result being a relentless four-day shellacking by the county prosecutor's office. If you didn't know better, you would have thought I lived to kill people the way those guys told it.

By the time the beating was over and the verdict was cast, my jury found me guilty of Assault In The First Degree, with a ten-year sentence; guilty of Assault On Law Enforcement In The First Degree, with a fifteen-year sentence; and guilty of Armed Criminal Action, with a five-year sentence. From there, my judge had the option of running the charges consecutively or concurrently. Consecutively meant I would have to complete each sentence one at a time (totaling thirty years), to where concurrently would allow for them all to be served simultaneously (totaling fifteen years). He chose to run the two assault charges consecutive to one another, while running the armed criminal action charge concurrent, giving me a twenty-five year sentence.

There was no rapping of the gavel, just the lifeless, steel words of a man completely indifferent to that which he had been elected to oversee. More than for my own sake, I hated this for my family. Some of the sounds coming from behind me can only be likened unto what you hear when someone gets punched in the stomach. Their guttural responses were nauseating, and looking back, what I saw only further testified to these pitiful noises. The wounded expression on my father's face, or the brokenness of my fragile baby sister, tears streaming down her cheeks. The older of my two little sisters, storming out of the court room in shattered teenage rebellion, telling the judge what she thought of him on her way out the door. My mother, unable to escape the harsh reality of her existence, as she helplessly buried herself into my stepfather. The shock of the rest of my extended family and friends who had endured through those long grueling days with me. It was a ruthless scene.

Yes, the outcome of my trial and the manner in which it was conducted was a perversion of justice, but the fact remains, I alone landed myself in that courtroom. Years of bad decisions had placed me in the hands of thoughtless people. Surely if I had grabbed hold of the reins sooner, I would have never tripped the wire that decimated my psyche. I would have never been where I was, to get me where I had gotten. But I had given my life to frivolous seed tossing, and now I was to reap.

Again, I cannot let the sun set on this chapter without glorifying the matchless name of Jesus. Yes, my trial, along with my sentencing may have been vicious blows, and my portrayal of the events may have been accurate, but really, they were mere stones being thrown at a mountain. Truly, only those who have an experiential knowledge of "the peace of God, which passeth all understanding" can relate to what I'm saying here. It literally surpasses ALL finite rationality to think of the peace and tranquility Jesus robed me in while going through such potentially devastating events. Yes, it hurt to bear the pain of my loved ones, and, yes, it hurt to have damaged the lives of innocent people, but even that was short lived, as I healthily embraced and processed the emotions, giving them to my Father.

To briefly sum up the whole ordeal, after sharing my remorse at my sentencing hearing, I concisely preached Christ and Him crucified to all who were present in the court room that day. In response, I was deemed a fraudulent hypocrite by my judge, accused of using my Savior's name as a manipulation tactic. Following his insults, he took it upon himself to usurp my jury's decision and sentence me to ten extra years in prison, crushing my family in the process. To this, I left the courtroom shackled and singing praises. At first, my song was gentle and private, but then the bailiff who was escorting me back to the jail told me to "shut up". The two of us were in the elevator, and wanting to be an obedient citizen, I zipped my lips. Then, Someone more important than the bailiff spoke, " Sing." From there, the bailiff got the *choir* version, rather than the *lay me down to sleep* version. Won't He do it?

ONE LIFE

"It is not the critic who counts, not the man who points out how the strong man stumbles or where the doer of deeds could have done them better.

The credit belongs to the man who is actually in the arena, whose face is marred by dust and sweat and blood, who strives valiantly, who errs and comes short again and again, because there is no effort without error and shortcomings, who knows great devotion, who spends himself in a worthy cause, who at best in the end knows the high achievement of triumph, and who at worst,

> *if he fails while daring greatly, knows his place shall never be with those timid and cold souls who know neither victory nor defeat."*
>
> — THEODORE ROOSEVELT

Well, my friend, as we part ways, I encourage you to *seize the day*. Whatever that may look like, it is worth doing. Whether your train is still on its tracks or you're reading from a place similar to the one I'm writing from, this is it for all of us. For better or worse, we've got one life to live, and right now we're living it. Yesterday is dead, and tomorrow may never be. Today is the day we have been given, and we would do well to give the day to love.

Love is the greatest of all experiences, and it is something all human beings were created to experience. Unfortunately, though, we as people often seek to receive love without also giving it, and this ends up creating a *lose-lose* situation. The truth is that we were created to *give* love just as much as we were to receive it, and when we fail to give, we also tie our hands when it comes to actually receiving this most precious of things. There is a divine ebb and flow to life's design, and only when fully participating can we experience life, as we were created to experience it. It is only when we selflessly give ourselves to those around us that we will be overwhelmed by what comes back to us. It is only when we love with everything we have that everything we have will be love.

As our own worst enemies when it comes to giving as well as receiving love, I have found the weapons we most commonly afflict ourselves with are fear and pride. Rather than giving and receiving in a symbiotic relationship with the world around us, we are all too often given to these two culprits, which are utterly toxic to love's existence. This is perhaps most evident in our fear of failure, as well as our fear of rejection. We effectively choke love out by living in the opinions of others, and in turn, by creating "comfort zones" for ourselves. We allow society to pawn its artificial version of fulfillment off on us, and we settle. We tell ourselves and seek to convince others, as well, that these zones are enjoyable, when in reality, they are places of confinement, deception, and misery. They provide a false sense of comfort, while robbing us of the real thing. We worry so much about what other people think that we never actually present our authentic selves for them to make a decision on.

For myself, along with many others, the *comfort zones* we create, involve substance abuse, but these zones are not at all limited to the use of drugs and alcohol. It would be a vast understatement to say the mass majority of people exist rather than live, and there are a hundred and one places people choose to do this. I will leave that part of the discovery up to you. I will, however, encourage you to be completely objective in your search. Remember that if we want something different, we must in fact try something *different*. More of the same will only produce more of the same. I wish I could offer something a little more profound, but it really is that simple. With objectivity and wholeheartedness accompanying the willingness to make a radical change, what we as human beings can achieve is limitless. Freedom beckons, and all we have to do is muster up the bravery and humility to accept the call.

I must warn, this is not easy. A life of love and loyalty is not for the faint of heart. In principle, it is very simple, but in practice, it is not at all easy. It requires devotion and determination. Love is more than pleasant feelings and emotions. It is more than physical infatuations, and it is more than giving hugs and handing out gifts to strangers. Love is a conscious decision that determines to do what is in the absolute best interest of the one being loved. We cannot claim to love someone or something, while at the same time choose not to faithfully live out that expression. At the cost of being sacrificial, love is selfless. It is patient, hopeful, kind, and enduring. It may not always feel good, but it is always true. Love is a labor, and it is one that is well worth its reward.

In closing, may I remind you that your past does not define you. No matter who you are and no matter what you have done, you are deserving of love. And if no one has told you lately that they love you, I love you. As a human being, you were created and fashioned with worth and value, and there are others in this world who would love to treat you as such. You are not alone, and you have a purpose far beyond your finite comprehension. There is only one you, and no one can do you better than you. So continue seeking, my friend. Continue seeking, and I promise you will find.

7

A MOTHER'S PERSPECTIVE

Throughout my life experience, nothing has triggered feelings of fear more than life's unknowns, and the late summer/early fall of 2011 was definitely a season of such. I will never forget walking into Scotty's hospital room. Though I had spoken with the hospital staff and briefly conversed with Scotty before arriving, nothing could prepare me for what I was about to witness. He looked so feeble, so out of touch with reality. I remember bringing his childhood blanket with me. Even though he was a twenty-one year old man, I knew from my conversation with him that he was in desperate need of some comfort. I thought the blanket would help, and it did. He noticed it immediately, and I walked over to the bed where he was lying to cover him up. The blanket brought visible comfort, and as he pulled it up to his neck, he asked, "Remember when you used to read to me?" He then informed me that just the night before he had read an entire chemistry book.

"Oh really." I responded, knowing this was not the case.

"Yes. As a matter of fact, I've read every book known to mankind in the past three days."

It was at that moment I knew how rapid Scotty's mind must have been firing. I was given a glimpse into how overloaded with information his brain was since overdosing on the LSD less than a week prior. To make a long story short, I was scared.

Over the course of the next three days, I never left Scotty's side. I would catch intermittent sleep in the bedside chair, but with Scotty not sleeping at all, I was mostly up. I witnessed some of the most bizarre behavior I had ever, or still to this day, have ever seen. At one point he thought he was giving birth, labor pains and all! I was mentally and emotionally exhausted, not to mention terrified of what the future might hold in store for my son. The doctor had shared with me that Scotty was suffering from a chemically induced psychosis, and after explaining what exactly this meant, she informed me that he may never come out of it. "He may be stuck like this forever." One can only imagine the panic and devastation a mother would feel at hearing such news. *The unknown.*

Paper itself could not contain all the things I witnessed from my son over the next seven months. He truly was the craziest person I had ever seen. Crazy as he may have been, though, he was also full of love, laughter, adventure, and creativity. There was never a dull moment, and I grew to love this new and crazy young man. I saw a light in him I had not seen since his childhood. I saw an intelligence in him I always knew existed, but just hadn't seen in several years. I witnessed a search for truth in him, and I admired it deeply. As crazy as he was, there were times when he seemed more enlightened to the truth of life than most other people I knew. I only hoped and prayed that a sense of normalcy would once again return.

Around March/April of 2012, we began to see light at the end of the tunnel. Scotty's sharpness was returning, and for the first time since his stay in the hospital, I believed he would one day be normal. Then came the horrific night of April 18th.

I thought I would die of sorrow. When our children are young, we can never imagine a life of drug addiction for them. We hope for the best, and then life happens. I wish I would have kept my head in the game. I wish I would have paid more attention to Scotty's needs during his young teen years and kept him safe the way a mother is supposed to do. What I wouldn't give to do it all over again.

I would love to be able to go back and right all my wrongs, but as we all know that just isn't possible. So instead, I choose to harness that pain and give it to God. I may not be able to turn back time, but I can use the time I have to serve and praise the God who has so graciously redeemed my son from the devastating life you have just got done reading about. I may never get a second chance to raise my children, but by the grace of God, I am given another chance every day of my life to learn from my mistakes and allow King Jesus to *bring beauty from my ashes*. The reaping process may at times be gut-wrenching, but through it all, our Heavenly Father is a God who will *restore the years the locust has eaten*. We just have to stay tuned to witness Him do so. Amen.

8

TREACHERY

I was raised in Truth from the time of my earliest memories. I was in church just about every time the doors were open and was born again by the time I was eight years old. There was something I desperately lacked, though—a personal and intimate relationship with Jesus Christ. I never knew this, because I never knew abstinence from the things of this world. My home life always afforded me to dabble, even if "only a little bit," and this caused me to be unfaithful before I ever knew what faithful was. Sure, I'd heard the terms "holy" and "worldly" more times than I could count, but I never had any real revelation of such concepts.

My mother fought a dogged fight to protect my sisters and I from the insidious influences of our sin-sick society, but unfortunately *"a little leaven leaveneth the whole lump."*[1] As a child, I was an athlete who played at a competitive level of sports. This being the case church and sporting events would often collide, and "play ball" it was. Sports taking precedent over church attendance combined with the constant bombardment of public school, I began living in the opinions of my worldly peers. I wanted to be cool, and no matter how small that box was, I was determined to fit inside of it.

By eleven, I was becoming loathsome of *mom's crazy church practices*, and by twelve, I was noticeably backslidden. Right around this same time, my parents' marriage was being thrown to the rocks, and amidst their struggles the vigorous discipline I'd always known began to slack. I thus began fulfilling, *"a child left to himself bringeth his mother to shame."*[2] Movies, music, video games, etc. that had all been strictly forbidden began to slither in, and at the time I couldn't have been happier. I was becoming a real life, bonafide Canaanite.

Drugs, alcohol, fighting, stealing, vandalism, promiscuity: these were tools of the trade. Long before they were vice grips on my soul, these were simply means to an end of fitting in as the baddest bad boy in school—something I was soon to drop out of all together. Just shy of my fifteenth birthday, my parents' marriage crumbled into divorce, and even mom (whom I thought to be the epitome of "Pentecostal") backslid. The lack of supervision became zero supervision, and before long school was out of the question.

Fast forward to sixteen, and mom was on her way to prison to complete a 120-day shock treatment on the count of one too many DWI's, and I was an atheist, sitting in a 60-day inpatient rehab center as my last step before being turned over to the state until I was an adult. After being released from rehab, I was sent to live with my dad. Him and mom thought that best, hoping maybe dad could get me on the right track. Unfortunately, this was not the case. Once close, my father and I had grown estranged and volatile. The two of us would spend the next four and a half years living together, and I'll just say our unresolved issues often manifested themselves in fits of unfortunate drunkenness. Thank you, Jesus. To know where I've been and to know where I'm at now is to understand why I must interject that here. Thank you, Jesus!!! Amen.

My teen years would swap out my dreams of playing college ball somewhere with full time criminality. I sold drugs as a primary source of income, while smoking weed and drinking daily—frequently using other drugs, as well. My life was a nonstop party, and no matter how many nights ended in repetitive dry heaves, chaotic violence, tear-filled self-affliction, or blackout oblivion, my lifestyle raged onward. I partied with anybody, anywhere, anytime, completely blind to the fact that I was simply trying to escape the reality that I was hollow inside.

Are we still having fun? By nineteen not so much. I'd been to more house parties, bars, and concerts than I could care to count, and the once bright lights of it all had begun to fade into one nonstop scene of been there, done that, more of the same. This is where my addiction to opiates slipped in. I'd never really cared for opiates in the past, because they make one to *nod off*, and I wanted to *rage*, not *nod*. However, as the two of us were reintroduced at this later date, I fell in love.

Oxycontin turned to heroin, heroin turned to the needle and spoon, and all of this translated into an addiction that only a fellow heroin addict can relate to. It is an existence that lives to witness the syringe fill with blood, the blood mix with the dope, and the mix be pushed back into the vein. From there we can function.

Selling drugs came very natural to me, and so once I began shooting heroin it only made sense to add that to my menu. The more you buy, the cheaper you get it, and the more you can do for free. The math of an addict. This meant I rarely had to deal with the sickness that plagues an addict who doesn't have their *fix*. So nope, no problems here. I mean why doesn't everyone shoot dope? Don't they know what they're missing? One hundred percent deaf, dumb, and blind to myself, I thought I had it all mapped out. I'll move to California where I can legally grow marijuana to supply *medical dispensaries*, and in the process grow poppy plants and learn how to produce my own heroin.

In July of 2011, at the age of 21, I returned from California to Missouri in order to get my high school sweetheart and head off to our new life together in the Great Redwood Forest. A dispute over money led to the two of us breaking up however, and we never made it back out west. Completely my fault. Once broken up she found out I'd been shooting heroin for the past year and a half behind her back, blaming it on *xanax* when I was still noticeably high once she was off work. This meant she wasn't coming back, and her not coming back drove me to a very dangerous place.

Okay, so you know the story from here. What you don't know, however, is the *whole* story. From this point forward, we will be diving into the spiritual depths of the nearly two-year journey that ultimately landed me at the foot of Calvary. For those of you unfamiliar with the *occult*, I am no expert, but I will be doing my best to share my own experiential knowledge, along with that which I have studied over the years. For some the contents of these chapters may sound even stranger than the already very strange events you've been reading about but let me assure you that the powers of darkness are as real as the book in your hands.

Along with glorifying the matchless name of Jesus, my hope in writing this expanded edition is to bring awareness to the satanic influence that has been gaining an increasing foothold in our nation over the past couple decades. Books and movies like *Harry Potter*, accompanied by the boom of social media, the normalization of drug use, and the overall spiritual erosion of our culture have played a vital role in setting the stage for witchcraft, eastern mysticism, and a whole hodgepodge mess of new-age, occult practices to flourish here in our Constitutional Republic.

Satanic possession is not just something mentioned in *Bible times* or portrayed by the film industry. In Paul's letter to the Ephesians, he labels Satan as *"the prince of the power of the air,"* and again in his second letter to the church at Corinth he refers to him as *"the god of this world."* When Adam chose to sin in the garden of Eden, he forfeited his God-given dominion over to Satan, and ever since then men have been *"taken captive by him at his will."*[3] Still to this very day lost souls all over the world are lured and deceived into the clutches of Satan, yielding their bodies as vessels for him and his minions to use, abuse, and accomplish all sorts of evil through. The Bible teaches us that just as it is the Spirit of God *"which worketh in you both to will and to do of His good pleasure,"*[4] so too is it Satan *"that now worketh in the children of disobedience"*[5]—the word *worketh* being the exact same in the original Greek.

It is my firmly held belief that there are many more people under satanic possession here in the United States than most people commonly realize. The instances of possessed captives contorting themselves into seemingly impossible positions, levitating off the ground, or snarling venomous blasphemy in different voices, etc. may not be commonplace, but I don't believe this negates the reality of satanic possession itself. Much like the fact that we see a relatively small percentage of devils cast out of people, I believe the reasoning for both is that here on our soil, people have developed a sort of symbiotic relationship with the spirits that hold them captive. There is such a great level of comfort afforded to the citizens of our country that it translates into a warped and false sense of comfort between host and parasite. In laymen's terms, we have been rocked to sleep.

In the chapters that follow, we will simply be revisiting and elaborating on the time period outlined in chapters three through five, beginning with the night of the liquid LSD. Once in, we will be in, though. So if you need to make yourself a cup of coffee go ahead and do it now. And for those of you who don't drink coffee, I suppose tea will do.

9

WITHOUT AN ANCHOR

"Now there was a day when the sons of God came to present themselves before the LORD, and Satan came also among them. And the LORD said unto Satan, Whence comest thou? Then Satan answered the LORD, and said, From going to and fro in the earth, and walking up and down in it. And the LORD said unto Satan, Hast thou considered my servant Job, that there is none like him in the earth, a perfect and upright man, one that feareth God, and escheweth evil? Then Satan answered the LORD, and said, Doth Job fear for nought? Hast not thou made an hedge about him, and about his house, and about all that he hath on every side? thou hast blessed the work of his hands, and his

> *substance is increased in the land. But put forth thine hand now, and touch all that he hath, and he will curse thee to thy face. And the LORD said unto Satan, Behold, all that he hath is in thy power; only upon himself put not forth thine hand. So Satan went forth from the presence of the LORD."*

> — JOB 1:6-12

There is much about the spiritual realm that the Bible leaves to the imagination, but at times we're given some very informative glimpses into the things unseen. What exactly the above quoted scene from the book of *Job* may have looked like, we may not know, but what we do know is that God and Satan have conversations about the lives of people here on earth. How often this happens, again, we do not know, but we do know that it happens, and ever since I first read this passage years ago, I have always felt as though something similar took place in my own life. Now at the time of what I believe to be the conversation about my own life, I was far from a *perfect and upright man*, but I believe a conversation happened just the same.

> *"And we know that all things work together for good to them that love God, to them who are the called according to His purpose. For whom He did foreknow, He also did predestinate to be conformed to the image of His Son, that He might be the firstborn among many brethren."*
>
> — ROMANS 8:28-29

I recently heard an illustration that described the entrance of heaven's gates as having a sign above them that reads, *"whomsoever will,"*[1] but once inside, one can look back and see a sign declaring, *"chosen before the foundation of the world."*[2] Without going too deep into doctrines of predestination and man's free will, I think this simple illustration sums it up quite well. In His infinite wisdom, God knows every choice we will ever make, yet the choice is still ours to make. He knows who His chosen are before we are ever even known of our parents, yet we still have to choose to know Him. God will move through both providential and supernatural means to get His elect where He desires them to be, yet even while He is moving on our behalf, we can be totally blind to

His existence. He may be opening doors we could never even fathom or welding doors shut that we have placed all our hopes and dreams in, and all the while we can be absolutely clueless to the reality that He is drawing us into our destiny. But the end result is always the same. Those who God has *chosen before the foundation of the world* always respond, and the Father's children always make it home for supper.

This brings us back to the afore mentioned conversation I believe was held in regard to my life here on this planet.

Satan knew I had been born again as a child. He was aware of the prophecies that had been spoken over my life. He had heard the many, fervent prayers that had been cried out on my behalf. Going all the way back to my mother's decision not to have me murdered in her womb, he had recognized God's hedge of protection preserve my life amidst numerous near-death experiences. And during the early fall of 2011, I believe he was put on notice by God that I would not be returning to California, but rather that I would be undergoing a spiritual awakening, being shaken from the coma I had been in for so many years. To this, I believe Satan responded with something like, "Allow me to wake him up. He's never really loved you anyway. Let me wake him up, and he'll serve me." And much like was the case with Job, I believe my Father granted his request. Whether or not I'm correct about this, I have no Divine authority, but however it went down, the outcome was me *waking up* on the wrong side of the spiritual bed.

Prior to having my eyes forced open, it wasn't just the existence of God I was blind to, but the spiritual realm altogether. I was a strict materialist, and a cynic toward anything having to do with the supernatural. Just as much as I thought people who believed in God were naive at best, I thought anybody practicing witchcraft or the likes was a certified weirdo. I believed only in the physical and pursued only that which brought instant gratification, which meant Lucifer had his work cut out for him if he were going to turn me into a satanist. For just as operating in the power of God requires faith, so too does operating in the powers of darkness.

Satan wasted no time in tearing down my walls of materialism. Beginning with amplifying my misery and revealing the harsh reality of my emptiness, he spun hallucination after hallucination, as outlined in the opening pages of chapter three. These hallucinations were not just random delusions, but rather strategic visions being burned into my conscious mind, each one building on the previous with purposed precision. He was demolishing my facade with the intent of rebuilding me for his own use. Much to his dismay, however, King Jesus was simply allowing *all things to work together for my good*.

After coming to Christ, a little over a year and a half removed from that fateful night in Dusty's basement, I would reflect back on some of the initial hallucinations I experienced, and I believe God gave me some valuable insight in the process. In particular, I would like to unpack the experience where I was pulled into my mind's eye for the twisted *time travel* of sorts (see Ch. 3). For the first twenty months after having had this experience, I had missed the deeper significance, focusing simply on the message the vision had conveyed to me that night. I now believe there was tailored reason behind every detail, and that the experience wrought something in me that was only subconsciously absorbed at first. I believe this vision was symbolic of my life, and that as I witnessed the images unfold before me, I was also being taken through a moral inventory of myself.

I would be lying if I tried to tell you exactly how long the whole experience lasted, but I do remember the part of the vision where I drifted into the future taking up just as much time as the rest of the vision in its entirety. I believe this was symbolic of the fact that at the time of the vision I spent my days *living in the future*. Unable to embrace the present due to unresolved issues from the past, I sought to escape by finding comfort in my grandiose hopes and dreams for the future. I had buried my past and numbed my present with facades and substance abuse and found my solace in what I thought would someday make everything alright. Thus, the bulk of the vision, which I believe to be representative of my life at the time, took place in the future. But as mesmerizing as *the future* was, it was not long before I was drug back into darker places.

Just as my literal past was an untreated and festering wound in my soul, so too were the scenes of *past times* far less pleasant than the bright and shiny objects of the future. From watching my parents arguing in their early twenties to witnessing numerous battle scenes from wars past, I was transported from one struggle to the next. I was being forced to endure the suppressed emotions and internal wars I had sought to escape for so many years, witnessing them manifest as tragic scenes in my mind's eye. As I shared in chapter three, I would occasionally cry out some shallow opinion in an attempt to stay tethered to the reality I had created for myself, which was simply a verbal testimony to my moral bankruptcy. Rather than having enough character to investigate and deal with the pain of life, I would blurt out superficial nonsense in a desperate attempt to escape. Clawing to get back to *the future*, I would argue with myself about who the greatest quarterback of all time was or something along those lines.

This experience came to a roaring climax when I went from visually and emotionally processing the vision to physically *becoming* the vision. As I detailed in chapter three, my physical body had become one with what I was witnessing, and as I was forced to face the fear of losing myself, I believe a literal destruction of who I had previously been was simultaneously taking place. I believe as I witnessed/felt the foundations of the earth being destroyed, so too were the pillars of my belief system crumbling into the dust of what once was.

With this insight, Satan's next stroke of evil genius becomes that much easier to understand. With a canvas as blank as a being lacking sovereignty could make it, he was able to paint an illusion of my dreams having come true (as outlined in Ch. 3), while at the same time convince me that this would only be achieved through spiritual means. With a subject as drug impaired and thus mentally compromised, as well as spiritually ignorant as I was, Satan had little trouble deceiving me with such methods. It was this type of crafty deception that came to define my daily existence, and thus it was that I went from being diabolically opposed to all things spiritual to the most spiritual person I knew overnight. Satan knew however, that he was never going to lure me in with things blatantly satanic, and so he came at me very subtly under the guise of *aliens*, *magic*, and *grandiose plans*. It was the *secrets of the universe* I was discovering, rather than outright devil worship.

For years, while living in sin, I had been a huge movie buff. So it should come as no surprise that Lucifer would manipulate this fact to his advantage when it came to baiting me in. The day after the Dub-Step Festival described in chapter three pt. 2 was a case and point example of this. It was further confirmation that I was *on the right path,* and along with being devastating, it was sadistically brilliant.

This would have been a Saturday and was my fourth day of no sleep. I was laying in my bed, lost in hallucination after hallucination, when everything came to a standstill and I heard, "Scott, you're dreaming. You've been training for this your whole life. Don't be afraid to dream a little bigger." Coming from one of my favorite movies at that time, these words were cleverly pulled from the film *Inception* and strung together for an audible experience from hell.

It all made perfect sense. This was why I had been sleeping in for twelve hours a day or so since I was a teenager. This is why I never remembered any of my dreams. It wasn't because I was lazy and depressed, or because I had been passing out rather than falling asleep since I was fifteen. No, the whole time I had actually been training for my destiny, and now the time had finally come for me to put my practice into action.

From seeing my brain light up after dosing my eyeball (convincing me pure LSD was the catalyst to all life's answers), to the monumental visions in Joey's basement, to the Dub-Step festival, to the universe's words from *Inception*, to finding Waldo, I was being swallowed whole by a leviathan. Not to mention the utterly indescribable physical sensations I was experiencing this entire time, accompanied by my own personal brand of bliss that served to be the constant mortar, solidifying the above-mentioned brick foundations to my delusions.

My spiritual depravity played a major role in everything that was taking place, but I would also like to share some insight into just why Satan was able to strike the way he did via my unusual amount of LSD use. You see, God has created human beings with natural guardrails in our minds that serve as an innate defense against the type of satanic activity described in this book. However, when we introduce mind-altering substances into our system, we lower these guardrails and weaken our God-given defenses, making us vulnerable prey to Satan and his unseen network of insidious spirits. Drugs and alcohol are not the only way to welcome these spirits in, of course, but they are very likely the most common method and one that is all too often overlooked and underestimated. This is exactly why the Bible warns us so many times against breaching our sobriety: *"Wherefore gird up the loins of your mind, be sober, and hope to the end for the grace that is to be brought unto you at the revelation of Jesus Christ...*[1] *Be sober, be vigilant; because your adversary the devil, as a roaring lion, walketh about, seeking whom he may devour."*[2]

SHIFTING GEARS

Subtle as ever, Satan made another strategic move shortly after I was released from the hospital (described in Ch. 3 Pt. 3). It was around nine in the morning, and I was sitting cross-legged in my buddy, Jared's front yard trying to communicate with the sun. With no real knowledge of such things, I was combining a sort of Buddhist hum with a Native American sounding chant and trying to change the color of the sun within my mind's eye. I felt like I was an incarnation of the sun here on earth, and that I needed to align with my *celestial self*. I was convinced this would be accomplished once I witnessed the sun turn purple. Mind you, I had never done anything like this in my life prior to this event, and it was all coming to me on the fly. Satanic inspiration.

Once achieving my goal of seeing the sun turn purple within my mind's eye things really ramped up. It were as though high-quality speakers had been turned on inside my head, and I began hearing the voice of a young woman named Katy Perry, *"Could you be the devil? Could you be an angel? Your touch, magnetizing, feels like I am floating leaves my body glowing, they say, be afraid, you're not like the others futuristic lover, different DNA, they don't understand you, you're from a whole 'nother world, a different dimension, you open my eyes, and I'm ready to go lead me into the light! Kiss me, ki-ki-kiss me, infect me with your lovin' fill me with your poison, take me, ta-ta-take me, wanna be your victim ready for abduction, boy you're an alien!"*[1]

I'm an alien. That's it!

Upon receiving this *revelation*, I immediately witnessed a lightbulb appear in my mind's eye. In HD clarity, there was a crystal-clear bulb that began to light up from either side of the base and connect in the middle at the top of the bulb. Literally, *a lightbulb had gone off in my head*, and if the song itself weren't a deal sealer, this little trick left absolutely no doubt—I was an alien. But I wasn't just any alien.

No, I was *could you be the devil? could you be an angel?* I was Lucifer.

From this day forward, if you would have met at a bar or a party or a checkout line in the grocery store, I would've introduced myself as Lucifer. And if our conversation would've stretched on for any real duration of time, I likely would've revealed to you that I was also *the sun god,* and that we were soon to be experiencing galactic interdimensional peace. Perhaps I would've even shared that aside from being me on earth and the sun in the sky, I also existed in my most powerful form as a massive, fanged beast, who had the form of a man with the wings of a dragon, cobras for dreadlocks, and the skin of a cuttlefish, with glowing neon tattoos swirling and changing all over my body—a being capable of creating and destroying galaxies, who had visited earth for a very special purpose. From changing my name and promoting this devilish nonsense on social media to seeking to *enlighten* everyone I met in person, I was *Lucifer the sun god,* and I was finally awakened to my purpose here on earth.

I cannot overstate the fact that aside from my Christian upbringing which had equipped me with the understanding that the devil was also a fallen angel, this was all brand new to me. I was clueless to the fact that there were actually other people on earth who worshipped the sun, as well as correlated *Lucifer the (alleged light) bearer* with being *the sun god*. I had no idea that there were circles within the occult who were also declaring that we were living in some special dispensation of time and that *nirvana* was just over the horizon. Nothing I was believing at this point was coming from study or research. It was all coming through spiritual intuition and undeniable experience.

I would also like to briefly clarify that I believe Lucifer and Satan to be one and the same being. Lucifer, Satan, the devil—I will be using these interchangeably throughout the book. I know there are different teachings when it comes to this topic, but this is what I believe the Bible conveys, and I just wanted clear up any potential confusion before going forward.

Lucifer's next overtly satanic maneuver would come a month or so after the morning in Jared's front yard. I was back to living with my father and was home alone, smoking a cigarette in the back bathroom. With no window and the light turned off, aside from the dull light bleeding in from down the hallway, the only illumination was coming from the cherry of my cigarette. Sitting on the counter and staring into the mirror, I was prompted to begin reciting an old summoning ritual I had encountered as a child. No sooner did the words leave my lips, and staring back at me was the face of a terribly aged and distorted witch of a woman. I remember a feeling of excitement coming over me. *It actually worked*! I thought. I watched in fascination for a few seconds, looking at what seemed to be her twisted howls of torment, and then decided to blow a cloud of smoke in her face. As the smoke dissipated, I was greeted with a new and different demonic figure. My excitement grew, and again I exhaled my cigarette smoke into the mirror, and again I was met with another face. I don't remember how many times I repeated this, but at one point, I remember swinging my hand up and tapping the side of my head, which caused the head in the mirror to disappear. I then swung my other hand up to tap the other side of my head, and another face appeared upon my previously headless body. At this, I laughed. It had become a game, and I was in control. *Or so I thought*. Eventually, however, things plateaued, and I got bored. Then came the punchline. I blew one more cloud of smoke into the mirror and with it, I made a challenge, "Mirror, mirror on the wall, show me the evilest face of them all." When the dust had settled, staring back at me was... me. It was my face in the mirror, only that it was symmetrically divided—half black and half white. *Could you be the devil? Could you be an angel?*

Once again, it all made perfect sense. The black and the white, the devil and the angel, the yin and the yang, the duality of who I was. This explained why even though I was now dedicated to love and peace, I also believed there were certain people who could not be forgiven and as a result, they would have to be eliminated. There was no middle ground—in or out. Even so, I never did identify myself as being *the devil*. Instead, I simply reasoned that Lucifer had been demonized. Perhaps it was my upbringing in the United States where most people root for the hero over the villain, but even during the throes of my possession, I always saw myself as combatting the devil rather than being the devil.

AFFIRMATION

In part three of chapter three, I described a little bit of what my life looked like in the months leading up to my arrest, while living with my cousin, Rodney. It was during this time that I started encountering occult beliefs outside of my own. Sailing the endless oceans of YouTube, my cousin and I watched everything from conspiracy theory videos on aliens living inside the moon to videos on the *gods* of ancient Egypt, and everything in between. But it wasn't just all the *new information* that fascinated me. What really got me was the fact that video after video corroborated a number of my own deeply held beliefs—beliefs I had received from the devil himself.

Along with some of my foundational beliefs being affirmed, like Lucifer being equated with the sun god (as well as *the good guy*) and aliens having visited earth in the form of human beings before, there were also some very minor details being affirmed. One example would be my *magic necklace*. This started on the night of the Dub-Step festival when I bought a wire wrapped quartz crystal. For some time leading up to that event, I had been wearing a thin, leather string with a small, metal Egyptian ankh hanging from it.[1] Hanging the crystal next to the ankh, I now had my *magic necklace*. Only it wasn't until delving into YouTube that I would be validated in having been proclaiming what many thought to be "Scotty's nonsense".

At the time that I began wearing the ankh, all I knew was I liked the way it looked. Same thing with the crystal. I had no clue these items were actually used by other magic practitioners within the occult. I may have been telling people that it was my *magic necklace*, but it wasn't until YouTube that I would realize just how accurate I had been. I would learn that the ankh traced back thousands of years, being a sacred and fundamental symbol in Egyptian black magic. Just as I would learn how important crystals were to a wide-ranging number of circles involved in witchcraft and the occult.

As I trekked the internet in search of *life's deepest secrets*, not only were my delusions being affirmed, but I was also becoming more and more fluent in the jargon of the occult. I was adding to my own mess by *connecting the dots* and picking and pulling from different videos, while at the same time learning to better articulate my outlandish ideas. As big of a role as the videos were playing, though, there was also the fact that the LSD was starting to wear off and Satan now had a more conscious vessel to work through.

A week or so after moving to the family property, I had another unforgettable experience. I had just found out my great grandfather had been a pedophile and words cannot describe the rage I felt at hearing this. Immediately, I wanted to somehow punish him. Explicitly, I wanted to resurrect him from the dead in order to decapitate him. Frustrated at how to go about achieving this, that's when I heard a very clear voice speak up in my spirit, "Hold a seance."

I don't know how to hold a seance. I thought.

"I'll teach you." Came the immediate response.

As we discussed in the tail end of chapter eight, "the spirit that now worketh in the children of disobedience" found in Ephesians 2:2 uses the same exact Greek word for worketh (energeō) that Philippians 2:13 uses when describing that it is "God which worketh" in believers in order to accomplish His will in their lives. On the night in focus, when I was *taught* how to hold a seance, the voice in my spirit sounded near identical to times when I've heard from the Spirit of God. This is precisely why John urges us in 1st John 4:1, "Beloved, believe not every spirit, but try the spirits whether they are of God..." We must be able to decipher between the voice of our flesh, the voice of a devil, and the voice of God. They may all sound very similar at times, but it is imperative that we discern the difference. We must be rooted and grounded in the Word of God, steeped in prayer, and sanctified through obedience to God's commands in order to avoid falling prey to voices of deception. Unfortunately, I was not, and therefore was deceived into thinking I was receiving divine guidance.

I will spare the details of the *séance* that was held, because the last thing I want to do is promote this type of demented activity. The things of Satan lead to death, despair, and ultimately to eternal damnation. I experienced many things that one may perceive to be *magic* or *paranormal*, but what they were was evil, and if not for the grace of God they would have been my demise. There is, however, one more story I would like to share from this season of my life, because with it, I believe comes some valuable insight.

It was sometime past midnight, and Eli and I were sitting out in my cousin Rodney's car, smoking some weed. I was telling him all about *life's origins*, and how the sun had mated with the earth in order to bring about creation (again, at the time, I didn't know there were other people who actually believed this nonsense, as well). Well, as I was sharing all of this, the two of us were greeted with an intense display of light. Out in the field, to our left was this massive sphere of radiating illumination, almost as if a full moon were emanating bright, white light, not fifty yards away from us. "Scotty, you're freakin' me out man. You're doin' it again!" Eli had been with me at the séance—hence, the "again".

How long this light appeared for, I can't recall. I just remember that it was much bigger and much brighter than lights like it I had previously seen. On two other occasions I had seen these strange orbs of light, but both times they were significantly smaller and much further away. The first two times I saw them, I thought they were UFO's (as did the other people I was with), and on the night being described, I simply thought it was *a sign from the universe* that my theory about creation was correct. I share all of this because I am now whole-heartedly convinced that these sightings were demons, and although I have not personally encountered any reporting or media coverage on these phenomenas, I would venture to say that there are people out there who are familiar with these types of lights and are trying to attribute them to *aliens*. I say this because I have met others in my relatively small social circle who have seen similar lights, and also because I know Satan likes to deceive people away from a biblical world view by using the whole *alien* theory as a scapegoat for demonic activity.

One of the men I know who has had similar encounters with these lights of darkness is a man I have met here in prison. Both of his accounts that I will be sharing took place in a Missouri prison known as "The Old Walls" or "the bloodiest forty-seven acres west of the Mississippi". The first account was something he witnessed on his way to the chow hall one evening. As he approached the cafeteria, he saw a string of lights above the door that he likened unto a string of old-school, multicolored Christmas bulbs. One by one, he witnessed these lights zip down from their position and go into different men as they entered the dining hall... *"taken captive by him at his will."*[2]

The second experience was an eerie event that transpired in the dead of night while everyone was locked in their cells. At around three in the morning, he was awakened by the howling, barking, and shouting of his fellow inmates. As he rose from his mat in confusion, what he saw was men on all four tiers shaking the bars in front of their cells, going wild as a large plasma-like ball of white light came passing through the prison. He believes the abnormally large size of this being was indicative of its status in the demonic ranks, and that the howling men were simply possessed vessels, rising to salute their military superior. I don't disagree.

We cannot underestimate the satanic activity in this country. From the subtle and insidious influences that permeate our culture, to the sacrifices in the woods, it is all around us, and we will never be able to effectively combat it if we do not adequately address it. As a culture, we have long been deceived by warped definitions of good and evil. Most everyone loves a good story where the protagonist defeats the antagonist, but very few people actually desire to live a life of righteousness capable of defeating the evil around them. We as an American people love the idea but are all too often unwilling to walk the walk necessary to make it happen. Our culture has been bamboozled by Hollywood's portrayal of the hero triumphing over the villain (with the *magic* of Disney being the greatest offender of all),[5] and as a result good and evil have become relative terms, subject to the whims and opinions of fickle people and their unstable emotions.

It is the church that God is wanting to work through in order to combat the darkness that saturates our society. He is wanting to work through you and me, and the time is now. We do not have time to compromise, fraternize, and flirt with the powers of darkness. We do not have time to blend in and fly under the radar. We have been called to push back. We have been called to scatter the darkness, as cities on a hill and lights of the world. Amen.

As we close out this chapter, I would like to put a bow on this period of my life by echoing the old cliché, *the road to hell is paved with good intentions*. My intentions were literally as good as they could possibly be from the fall of 2011 into the spring of 2012, when I almost took the lives of multiple people based on these intentions. This is because good intentions are not what determines good behavior. Good behavior is objectively defined by God Almighty's standard of righteousness, which is only discovered in the truth of Christ Jesus, as revealed in the Holy Bible. Aside from that, good intentions are ultimately sugar-coated poison. Righteousness—that is what we are after.

That being said, I do not want to diminish the pursuit of love that I began during this time. For although love cannot be accurately expressed or experienced aside from God's truth, when pursued with all diligence, love will eventually lead one to the Author of such a lofty treasure. The desire must be refined through the fires of life, having all dross of false notions burned out, but when cried after from the soul, the Father will always respond. It was this desire and desperate pursuit that pushed me through the insanity of my darkness. For *God is love*[3] and *love covereth all sins.*[4] Amen.

From here, we will head into St. Charles County Jail —my favorite place on earth.

12

GLORY, HONOR, POWER AND PRAISE FOREVER, AMEN.

In chapter five, I shared how important my time spent in St. Charles County Jail was, even before my conversion. What I didn't share, though, was how at the same time I was developing my character, I was also still wading around in some very dark spiritual waters. My Luciferian propaganda was still in full effect, as was my reading into various belief systems for *key pieces to life's puzzle*. Between scavenging the jail's bookshelf for spiritual material and having my mom (who was still backslidden, as well) mail me in printouts on whatever new practice I was interested in, I was continuing on the same exact journey I had been on prior to the horrific night of April 18th. The only differences were that I didn't have YouTube or Rodney by my side, and I no longer thought LSD was a key part of the equation.

Of all the beliefs I was digging around in, Christianity was not one of them. I had bought the lies concerning Christianity lock, stock, and barrel, and viewed those who believed as gullible and naive. I had been jaded from hypocrisies in the church since I was a boy, and theories pointing out *contradictions* and *conspiracies* in the Christian religion just added ice to the tundra. This brings us to our next scene in H-Pod of St. Charles County Jail.

It was a Sunday afternoon, and as was the custom, a volunteer from a local church was in the day room holding a service with the ten or fifteen men who wanted to be present. I myself was far too *enlightened* to be partaking in such things, and thus chose to stay in my cell, just as I did every week when these services were being held. On this particular Sunday, however, I heard something coming from the service that demanded my attention.

"You'll never achieve freedom of the mind outside of Jesus Christ!" The preacher was a demonstrative man who was sharply dressed and very charismatic. He was animated with excitement, as he proclaimed freedom through Christ alone, and I could hear him all the way from my cell. His words of truth were like nails on a chalkboard, and immediately following his declaration, I heard something much more insidious. In near identical fashion to the music I heard while sitting cross-legged in Jared's front yard, chanting to the sun, I heard the lyrics, "Don't help them to bury the lie..." coming from the old rock band, *Pink Floyd*. He was lying to my people. I had to act.

Immediately, I pressed the intercom button in my cell to get the attention of the guard in the control center. He responded by asking if everything was alright, and I told him everything was fine and asked if he would slide my door open (we had electric doors that slid open and shut on tracks), so that I could go downstairs and join the service. He obliged, and what followed would have implications reaching further than I could've ever imagined.

Joining the small group, the preacher's attention was turned to me, and I wasted no time in confronting him. "I heard you say that Jesus was the only way to achieve freedom of the mind."

"Yes." The preacher's simple statement was sincere, as he nodded his head and smiled at me.

"Well, you see, preacher, I've achieved freedom of the mind."

"Good. So, you know Jesus." Again, he was sincere and totally unaware of where our conversation was going.

"That's the thing. I've done it *without* Jesus Christ." My words were now dripping with obvious pride and evil.

"The devil is a liar." The preacher's countenance had hardened, and his words were stern. Turning his attention to the other inmates, he tried to reel things back in, but the spirit in me wasn't done yet.

"Hold on. This isn't about them, or the devil, or anyone else. This is about me and my salvation." My tone had gone from arrogant to aggressive, and the volume was rising. "I've been searching for God high and low for the past year and a half of my life, and if Jesus Christ is the answer, then let me be shown! Let me be brought to my knees in tears of repentance! But if not, if my view of God is correct, well, then I know you're familiar with the story of Elijah, and the words that are about to come out of my mouth are going to be on fire. And if your view is correct, and Jesus is the answer then let my words be stopped and let me be brought to my knees in tears of repentance. But I think the words about to come out of my mouth are going to be on fire."

What happened next was a display of pure evil. Rapping at maximum decibel, I began spewing forth a filthy string of rhymes that consisted of Christian hypocrisies, Catholic crusades, conspiracy theories, and *new-age* concepts promoting the *true* path to peace, love, and enlightenment. It was all quite intense, and as I ranted, the preacher held up his Bible and repeated, "The devil is a liar! The devil is a liar! The devil is a liar!" as he left out of the pod. This was early 2013—February, I believe.

Come May of 2013, push was coming to shove. As I shared in chapter eleven, I was at the crossroads of *ascend or die trying*. I was done with philosophies, theories, and plans for the future. I had been banging against destiny's door for over a year and a half straight, and was going to get an answer, one way or another. Then something happened.

At the time of this incident, I was staying in cell twenty-two. I had been in cell twenty-two for a year and had in fact turned twenty-two while living there. One of the things I liked about this particular cell was the artwork on the walls. The off-white, concrete blocks were covered in pencil drawings done by the cell's previous inhabitants. All four walls were decorated from the floor to the ceiling, and included in these hodgepodge murals were numerous Christian drawings. There was an elaborate cross, a descending dove, a quote stating, "The hand of God felt here on 6/2/2011," etc. and even though I wasn't a Christian these drawings never bothered me—until they did.

No longer could I view these words and symbols as well-intentioned naivety. They were born of outright lies meant to deceive and oppress the masses, and I could no longer tolerate them. Angered by the thought of such widespread deception, as well as irritated at myself for having let it linger for so long, I soaped up a washcloth and took it to everything associated with the Christian faith. From there, I began replacing these sacred markings with my own religious symbols and *philosophical* quotes.

I was about halfway done with a 3 ft. Egyptian ankh, when out of nowhere the bottom of my toilet started gushing water. Seeing this, I hurriedly grabbed up my books and papers off the ground and hopped up onto my bunk. Pressing the intercom button, I informed the guard in the control center what was happening, and he told me to pack up my stuff and head to the cell next door. This would have been cell twenty-three, and the guy who had been living there had just left earlier that morning. It was also the cell where I would turn twenty-three years old.

Once in my new cell, I immediately went to work scrubbing the walls. For nearly two days, I spent the bulk of my free time turning my new cell into a clean canvas for me to express my own creativity on. Finally, all the unwanted graphite was erased, and once again, I set out drawing my own symbols—this time starting with a large anarchy sign, probably 2 ft. in diameter. This would have been somewhere around two or three in the morning, and never in my wildest imaginations could I have prepared for what was about to happen next.

Taking a break from my drawing, I walked over to my sink to get a drink of water. Staring into the scuffed stainless-steel mirror, I was for the first time since calming down after that initial phone call with my mom hit with some feelings of vulnerability. I had been so confident in my delusions and so out of touch with reality that I never thought about my situation from a negative perspective or considered the implications of possibly spending the rest of my natural born life behind bars. I wasn't facing life in prison, I was on my way to *ascension*. This night was destined to be different, though.

Wondering about what the future might hold in store, I went from looking over the physical countenance of my face (which at this time was framed by an unkept beard and dreadlocks) to staring myself in the eye, searching my soul for desperately needed answers. It was at this point that all peripheral facial features disappeared, and the image before me turned to an utter abyss of complete blackness. *You have a demon in you.* This was not the first time I had experienced the abyss in the mirror, and it was not the first time I had been met with this same exact thought when it happened. The other couple of times had happened before coming to jail, and both times I had casually shrugged off the notion of being possessed, chalking it up to just having done too much acid. Again, this night was destined to be different, though.

You have a demon in you. Rather than dismissing this thought as incredible, I thought just maybe, *Lucifer*. Upon considering the potential of this foul being who I had become so intertwined with actually being an insidious parasite rather than my true self, the abyss in the mirror began to swirl with smoke-like wisps. Sucked in with intrigue, I instinctively opened my mouth in awe and disbelief at what seemed to be happening. My voice was just above a whisper, "Lucifer?"

Instantaneously, the void of the abyss was filled, and I was face to face with a pale, gaunt, hideous being, with a white, clammy countenance and sunken in, black, beady eyes. My blood turned to ice. Unlike the instance in my bathroom mirror a year and a half prior, I was not at all feeling humored or empowered. I was petrified, and tried escaping the reality of what was happening with panicked thoughts of, *No, there's no such thing as the devil. It's all about the inner good. It's all about getting down to the inner good...*

"So you are all that's wrong with the world; you are going to accomplish my mission while you're here." Coming from my own mouth, these words from Lucifer were spoken with a hint of surprised satisfaction.

No, I'm about peace. I'm about love. Again, my thoughts were frantic, and as I tried refuting Satan's accusations, my claims of love and peace immediately birthed thoughts of none other than the Lord Jesus

Christ. *No, Jesus can't be the answer. That's kiddy stuff. I've come way too far for it to be that simple.*

Knowing his time was short, Lucifer made one more last-ditch effort. "You'd better grab your Bible, boy." Playing on my pride with a sort of reverse psychology, he taunted me with this statement (again, coming out of my own mouth), hoping just maybe I would resort to my self-assurance, responding with something like, "Bible? I'm a grown man. I don't need a Bible. This is all a joke." Only at this time in my life, my language would have been much more colorful. Colorful or not, though, this was not the case. I was taking everything that was transpiring at face value, and in scared desperation, I thought grabbing my Bible sounded like a pretty good idea.

For reasons I'll describe here shortly, I still had a little, worn, white, bonded leather, King James Version Bible that a man had given to me months prior. So without hesitation, I called Satan's bluff, and hurried over to my bunk to grab my Bible. Returning to the mirror, Bible in hand, Lucifer was still there staring back at me. I never even contemplated my next move. The Holy Ghost I had received as a child roared to life, and looking into the face of that old snake, I shouted, "Lucifer! In the name of Jesus Christ, get thee behind me!"

He vanished.

Talk about terrified. No longer was I staring the mere devil in the face—I was now dealing with a Being much more severe. I was an unrepentant soul in the presence of a Holy God. Immediately, I began tearing up all the songs and books I had been working on and flushing them down the toilet. Along with my own writings, there was a book that had been particularly special to me that I began destroying. In this book, the author documents his conversations with numerous *angels*, ultimately climaxing with his conversations with *Lucifer*—conversations that were all too familiar.

The destroying of my prized literature was necessary, but really it should have been secondary. My repentance was the primary matter at hand, and I was stalling. So once I was done with the temporary distraction of flushing everything, I was back to square one. As powerful as what I had just experienced had been, though, my pride was proving to be even more influential. *If I admit Jesus is the answer, I'll have to tell everyone I've been wrong this whole time.*

Insanity! The pride of man is absolutely INSANE! I had literally just cast out Satan, in the Mighty Name of Jesus, and as a result had destroyed a year's worth of continual and treasured effort. Still, I couldn't bring myself to cry out to Jesus, in humble repentance. Instead, I was worried about preserving my crazed and deranged self-image. Unable to reconcile what all was becoming blatantly clear by simply talking to God about it, I instead did everything I could to avoid thinking about Him. I hid from Him —much like Adam and Eve, thousands of years before me.

Seeking some sort of comfort and relief, I remember laying down on my mat and clutching that little Bible to my chest. Comfort and relief were impossible, though. I was terrified, and all I could think was, *If I die, I'm going to hell.* God is merciful, though, and eventually, He allowed me to fall asleep.

Much like was the case when God and Satan conversed over my life at the time that I dropped all the LSD, I believe another conversation was held the night you've just finished reading about. I believe God told old Lucy that his time of leading me blindly along had come to an end. He had been given the time he had originally asked for, and he had failed to win my soul in the process. Sure, he had played magnificently on the lusts of my flesh—he had tricked, deceived, and lured me down a dark trail of spiritual weirdness—but he had failed at turning me into a satanist. He was never going to convince me to harm children or engage in human sacrifice or participate in homosexual rites or even openly declare "devil worship" for that matter. And during the wee morning hours of May 23, 2013, I believe he was once again put on notice by my Father, "Your time deceiving him is up. Tonight, he will see you for who you are, and he will see Me for who I am, and he will choose. But no longer will he follow you, thinking he is following Me. It ends tonight."

The next morning, when I woke up and made my way downstairs for breakfast, I was no more at ease than I had been when I had fallen asleep. The discomfort of conviction was blaring. I had to do something.

After finishing my pancakes and cheerios, I remember capitalizing on an opportunity that had been created the night before, just next door to me. A few hours before everything began cascading in my own cell, the medics had been called to my neighbor's cell. He had been violently throwing up, and the medical staff had spent quite a while with him, once showing up to his cell. This man's name was J.R.

After I had finished eating, I spotted J.R. and knew he was my *in* to pray. I may not have been humble enough to pray for myself, but I knew some praying needed to be done, and surely this elderly gentleman who had been so sick just the night before was the perfect candidate. My approach was both frank and sincere. "J.R., I heard you throwing up last night. Do you believe in the power of prayer?"

J.R. told me he did believe in the power of prayer, and that he would like for me to pray with him. This, of course, perked up the ears of a couple of nearby believers. *Scotty wanting to pray? What?* They too wanted to join in, and the four or five us gathered in a small circle and linked hands. What happened next would prove to be the greatest moment in my entire life. For the first time in a very long time, I began to pray in the name of Jesus, acknowledging Him as the God of all creation. Opening my prayer with that Precious and Almighty Name, "In the name of Jesus..." was all I got out. All at once, I was struck with the undeniable reality of who Jesus was. Immediately, I collapsed to my knees, burying my face in the floor and sobbing uncontrollably, as the love of God became the realest thing I'd ever known. "I'm sorry! I'm sorry! I'm sorry!" That was all I could slobber out. I had been ashamed of Jesus as a boy and denied Him, I had cursed Him and forsook Him as a teenager, I had blasphemed Him as an adult, and yet there He was. There He was in all His radiant glory, saving my wretched soul in some filthy, county jail day room. PRAISE—HIS—HOLY—NAME!!! HALLELUJAH!!!

As the old preacher once said, "If that don't light your fire, your wood's wet!" Amen! Wet as my wood may have been, it's been dry and blazin' ever since that fateful morning, on May 23, 2013. After I was finally able to pick myself up off the floor, I just wanted to be alone with Jesus. I went to the window at the control center and asked the guard to open my cell for me. Once inside, I just began to sing and dance and praise the Lord! I didn't know a single full song, but I began singing every string of lyrics I could remember. Truly, "*where the Spirit of the Lord is, there is liberty,*"[1] and I had a wonderful time in the Holy Ghost, right there in my cell (and still do to this very day, regardless of what cell I may be living in)!

If all this weren't enough, Jesus had yet another very personal, very mouth dropping surprise in store for me. After lunch, I was walking laps around the pod (as was my custom to walk a mile after lunch) when I felt the Holy Ghost stop me. "Where are we?" His voice was loud and clear.

I don't know, the place where they hand the meds out? I thought. Then it dawned on me, *This is where it happened! This is where You rescued me!*

"What else happened here, though?" Again, the Spirit of God was crystal clear. This time, it might have taken a second, but when it hit me, it hit me like a ton of bricks. Right there, in that exact same spot— the same exact spot where I had collapsed to my knees in tears of repentance was the EXACT same spot where I had challenged that preacher with such venom, just a couple of months prior, "If Jesus Christ is the answer, then let me be brought to my knees in tears of repentance!" Yeah.

Alright, so, let's rewind to why I even had a Bible in my possession on the night just described. I mean it would make sense that if I had been scrubbing my walls of all things Christian, then I surely wouldn't be lugging a Bible with me in my move next door. Well, if we go back a few weeks, we arrive at a scene where I am laying in my bunk and reading a Sci-Fi novel. The storyline to this particular novel was one where earth's resources had been destroyed by the carnage of war, and as a result, a remnant of humans had traveled to a nearby planet in hopes of starting over. Fast forward generations into the future on this new planet, and mankind was once again disintegrating into a state of self-destruction. From there, an unlikely hero arises to rally a small group of people together who set out to make a voyage back to earth and save the human race for a second time. In order to return to their home planet, though, they will need *earth's memories* which have been digitally stored onto a long-hidden device known as *the codex*. Well, as I was reading about this *codex*, the Holy Ghost (unbeknownst to me at the time) quickened me with the notion, "This kinda sounds like the Bible." And just like that, the Bible became a mystery worth holding onto.

It has often been said that "God will meet us where we're at but loves us too much to leave us there." How true these words are. At the time I was reading that novel, I had no desire whatsoever toward the

Word of God, but that mattered precious little to the desire that God had toward me. He knew He could speak to me louder through some whacked out science-fiction novel than He could through His most devout preacher of righteousness, and so that's exactly what He did.

Won't He do it?

ALL JESUS

From the moment of my repentance onward, it has been ALL JESUS. My transformation was immediate, radical and by the grace of God, enduring. My roots of having been raised in the Truth and born again as a child played a vital role in my early development, and things that had laid dormant for so many years suddenly sprang to life. Things that had been downloaded during my childhood—things I'd previously been unable to see—became instantly visible and plainly understood. These lessons that had been stored in my subconscious mind were immediately transferred to my conscious understanding and without hesitation became my uncompromising moral constitution.

Through the duration of my incarceration, God's grace has never failed me once. From then to now, He has affirmed His Word, shown His mighty hand, and blessed me beyond all reasonable measure. He alone has raised me, placing key people—wonderful people, as well as sandpaper people—in my path along the way. He has been my Savior, my Comforter, my Peace, my Sustainer, my Joy, my Strength, my Teacher, my Disciplinarian, my Coach, my Healer, my Best Friend, and so much more. He has been and will always be my Heavenly Father.

I could never, in all of eternity, overstate how good God has been to me. He has blessed me with my beautiful wife and helpmeet. My family relationships have been restored and strengthened. My mother is back to serving the Lord, stronger than ever. Her husband, my brother has as a result been saved, and the two of them minister beautifully together. My father and I are closer than ever and grow closer as the years go by. I've seen men in this prison house healed, filled with the Holy Ghost, baptized in Jesus' precious name, changed, delivered and ministered to. I've been blessed to share this same story more times than I could possibly remember, and by the grace of God plan on sharing it til the day the good Lord calls me home!

As I close out, there is one final lesson I have learned that I would like to share with you. Along with a daily determination to read the Word of God (whether I feel like it or not) and a conscious decision to continually cultivate a fervent prayer life, what I am about to share with you is what I believe to be the foundation to a successful walk in Christ Jesus. This is a slightly edited copy of an email I sent to a young man I was helping to disciple some months back:

> *"And I saw heaven opened, and behold a white horse and he that sat upon him was called Faithful and True, and in righteousness he doth judge and make war."*
>
> — REVELATION 19:11

I love this verse—one of my absolute favorites! This is Jesus. Yes, He became the suffering servant for our pitiful sakes, but HE IS the righteous Judge of ALL creation! HALLELUJAH!!!! GLORY HALLELUJAH, AND MAY ALL CREATION BOW TO HIS HOLY PRESENCE!!!

I don't know a lot, but one thing I'll never doubt is that Jesus loves me, and for me, that's enough. It's enough to demand my allegiance and fuel within me a reciprocal love that I guard with jealous tenacity. He who is everything gave everything for me, and for me that's enough.

The Bible makes it clear that love without obedience is not love (namely John 14:15). How can I fool myself into believing I love the King who became a sacrifice to become my friend if I do not obey His commandments? Has He not given me of His own Spirit to equip me to do so? I don't want to oversimplify it, but it really is that simple. We love Him, because He first loved us.

The Bible is a book of war. Even in the New Testament where love is the highlighted emphasis, we are continually reminded of life being one of warfare. We are exhorted to behave ourselves as soldiers. Only now we wrestle not against flesh and blood, but against principalities, and powers, and rulers of darkness, and spiritual wickedness in high places. This ties directly into obedience. We love our Commander—we trust Him—and thus we renounce everything that opposes His command. No questions asked. Yes, Father.

That's it. We determine that we love the Lover of our soul, and then we walk in His power to stand on it. And when we do that, we will stand in the face of Nebuchadnezzar, in the den of lions, or in the face of whatever temptation this life may bring our way. Does this mean we are perfect? No, but we do not sin willfully. We learn from our shortcomings, and we correct. It's not always easy, but it really is that simple. Determine you're going to love Jesus, and anything that dares get in the way of that gets removed immediately. Amen, and in Jesus' Mighty Name, Amen!

Well, my friend, thank you for taking the time to accept the invitation into my life. I plan to one day publish a book, sharing all the lessons and testimonies Jesus has blessed me with during my time behind the wire, in the meantime, suffice it to say that *"with man this is impossible, but with God all things are possible."*[1] No matter what this life may throw our way, *we are more than conquerors through him who loved us and gave himself for us.* All he is looking for is someone who will love him back. Will you be that someone?

WORD OF MOUTH IS THE NUMBER ONE WAY BOOKS ARE PROMOTED. SO IF YOU HAVE ENJOYED WHAT YOU'VE READ SO FAR, PLEASE TELL A FRIEND!

14

BROTHER AND SISTER SCOTTY DAVIS

Hold the phone! You may be wondering, and so here it is that I will oblige :) On account of my beloved wife informing me that nearly everyone who reads this book immediately follows up by asking her how on earth it is that the two of us came to be, I have decided to add this chapter and bring you up to speed!

It all began to manifest back in the summer of 2015 when Kayla and my mother first met. The two recognized their kindred spirits and became instant best friends. What they did not recognize, however, was that God was orchestrating something even greater than the very precious friendship they were beginning (although some family members and close friends have said that they knew immediately upon meeting Kayla that God had destined the two of us to be together).

Being unmarried and incarcerated, my mom was my closest friend, and the two of us talked at length over the phone on a daily basis. I can still remember my initial thoughts when she first told me about Kayla. Hearing her describe this beautiful, praise-singing, Apostolic, new best friend of hers (who just so happened to be my age), I couldn't help but feel a nudge of possibility deep within my spirit. At the time, however, Kayla had a boyfriend, I was serving a lengthy prison sentence, and the prospect was quickly dismissed. I was actually quite resolute that if God never reconciled Ashley and I, I would likely live a life of celibacy, consecrated unto the Lord, much like the apostle Paul. God, of course, had other plans.

After having started a "ladies' day" Bible study/time of fellowship with Kayla, my mother, and Kayla's grandmother (sister Zola), the three of them developed an intimate friendship, and my mom filled them in on her incarcerated son. Hearing about how my mom would frequently drive up to the prison to visit me, Kayla and Zola said that they would love to join her sometime. This was how

Kayla and I very first met. It was the spring of 2016.

I remember the first time I laid eyes on my lovely wife to be, I was dumfounded. As I approached the 4-person table where Kayla was sitting with my mom and her grandmother, I just remember being very caught off guard. Smitten as I may have been, though, I leaned into the power of the Holy Ghost, prayerfully dismissed any thoughts of potential romance, and greeted her with a handshake as a sister in the Lord. I actually spent the majority of the 4-hour visit focusing my eyes on my mom and sister Zola, making occasional eye-contact with Kayla simply to avoid seeming rude or awkward. In the end, the four of us shared testimonies, sang, prayed, and had a blessed time of godly fellowship.

Naturally thoughts of *what could be* tried flooding my mind as I walked back to my housing unit that evening, but again, I dismissed them as inappropriate and just thanked God for the two ladies who had been willing to come and visit a brother in the prison house. Kayla's boyfriend at the time, however, did not know my devotion to the Lord or the innocency of our visit, and was uncomfortable with Kayla continuing to come up with my mom and sister Zola. I shared with my mom that I completely understood and asked her to assure Kayla that I was not offended and that I was simply thankful she had been willing to come up in the first place. Despite Kayla no longer being allowed to join the two of them, sister Zola continued to accompany my mother every six weeks or so, and the two of us developed a deep and treasured friendship over the years.

Over the next year and a half, I rarely thought of Kayla, and when I did it was usually in the context of my mom requesting prayer for her or her being over at the house when I called home. Then came early January of 2018. It was around 9:30 at night, and as was our custom, my mom and I were on the phone praying. Kayla had been one of the people we were praying for, and as we began to pray for her in particular, I was overwhelmed with unprecedented feelings of love. Confused and taken aback by the experience, I shoved it aside and continued praying for the need at hand. Then as my mother and I were about to get off the phone something else unique happened. In closing, my mom said a prayer over my own life, and in it she included a petition for God to grant me "something special" that night.

After getting off the phone, I didn't think anything else about the feelings I had experienced when praying for Kayla. I simply headed back to my cell to lock down for the night. Fast forward to around 11 o'clock, and I was ending my night with some more intercessory prayer. Per usual, I was in my bunk praying for different people and needs as their faces would pop into my mind's eye. This had been going on for some minutes when Kayla popped back up. This was not necessarily an anomaly nor was it a regular occurrence. What made it an anomaly, however, was the fact that I was once again met with intense thoughts and feelings love! And once again, I tried dismissing them. Only I couldn't! I tried escaping the feelings by attempting to pray for anyone or anything else I could think of. Only I couldn't! It were as though God had boxed be into this little room, and He was not going to let me leave until I addressed it. So I took a deep breath and asked, "Okay, Dad, what's going on?"

Immediately, He posed back, "What if this is the woman I have created for you?" His response only added to my uneasiness. Like I shared before, I was quite convinced that if I were ever to take a wife, it would be because God had reconciled Ashley and I. More than anything else, I had this deep sense that since she alone had been there for the worst of me, she alone should get the best of me. However, after a little wrestling in my spirit, I submitted unto the Lord, desiring His will above all else. It was there in that sweet moment of embrace that I realized in crystal clarity God's destined plan for Kayla and I. The whole thing became undeniably plain as day, and I was flooded with the revelation of how God had brought our paths together, how compatible the two of us were, how deep of a friendship I had developed with her grandmother (who was like a second mother to her), and how the deep nudge I had always felt and just as quick dismissed was Him all along. For fifteen or twenty minutes, I was consumed with indescribable love and joy and revelation! It really was one of the most surreal and spiritual experiences of my entire life. So much so that when I came to from the experience, I had to use the restroom, and I just remember cracking up laughing at having to do "earthly" things. Of course this was around midnight, so I was doing my best to crack up quietly, as not to wake my cellmate.

A deep love was immediately birthed for this woman. It was not an "in love" love, because I really did not even know her, but it was an unwavering and godly love that held her in the prioritized position reserved for one's spouse. With this love came a responsibility, and with the responsibility came a burden. Back in my bunk, the weight of this burden shifted the atmosphere from light and joyful to heavy and aching. I was taken to a deeper and more fervent place of intercession than I had ever been before, and for the next however long, I wrestled in the spiritual realm and prayed for my wife. Of course, at the time all of this was happening, Kayla no longer had a boyfriend—just in case anyone was wondering.

The next morning I told my mom all about my experience, and she was in agreement that if it were truly God's will then it would doubtlessly come to pass. I might also add that none of this was unbelievable to me, because this was the sort of thing I would expect from God when it comes to Him informing His people of who He has chosen for them to marry. Having read the testimonies of brother and sister Tekel and Erkenesh, as well as brother and sister Goss (which I HIGHLY recommend you read their stories in *Unseen Hands* and *Winds of God*), this experience seemed very logical to me. I have never, since coming to the Lord, been a believer in the secular practice (and all too often church norm) of dating, so I was very comfortable with this method God had used. That being said, I was also very cautious to remain in the will of God every step of the way. Of course, I wanted to reach out to Kayla that very day and inform her of our heavenly arrangement, but I was sensitive to be patient and wait on God to open the door in His time and not mine. The days, weeks, and months that followed were filled with me being very prayerful, continuing to pray for Kayla as though she were in fact my destined help meet, while also caveating all my prayers with, "God, if I'm wrong about all this and I'm in my flesh, please show me! I beg you, do not let me be deceived in this!"

Eventually I broke the news to sister Zola. As Kayla's grandmother, I wanted her blessing in the matter, and so during a visit with her and my mom, I laid it all out. A bit nervous but led of God, I stepped out in faith and told her everything I believed God had been doing. I explained to her in detail the experience I had been given, as well as the nature of my prayers following that glorious night. She listened intently, and after hearing me out and prayerfully considering the situation, she told me that she would be okay with me taking her granddaughter's hand in marriage and that she thought I would be good to her. She assured me that she would be in agreement with my mother and I, that if it was in fact the will of God then it would come to fruition in His due time.

Finally, God's due time arrived. I had been given the experience in the beginning of January, and come late April, God was giving me the green light to reach out to *her whom my soul loveth*. He prompted me to write her a letter, presenting myself in complete transparency, and after making one-hundred percent certain I was not operating in my own understanding, I prepared to do so. I asked my mom to ask Kayla if it would be okay if I wrote, and once I received permission, I put pen to paper. I explained at length everything I had been experiencing over the past 4 months and what all I believed God had been communicating to me. Ultimately, I left her to believe I was either hopelessly delusional or that I was the man of her dreams (included at the end of the chapter is a copy of what my dear wife refers to as the "letter of all letters").

Before handing the narration over to my beloved wife, I would like to explain a little bit of the lead up to her receiving the letter, giving some insight into what all God was doing behind the scenes. I wrote the letter and mailed it out on a Thursday, meaning it should arrive to Kayla the following Monday.

Well, unbeknownst to me, it just so happened that Monday was also the day Kayla was scheduled to be wedding dress shopping with some of our friends and family for a mutual friend's wedding with my cousin. So as the letter was waiting in her mailbox, she was being consumed with thoughts of all things newlywed and uttering prayers for God to send her a husband. And with that, I will pass the mic to sister Davis.

Hi, everyone! This is Kayla, here to tell you about the *letter of all letters*! So I knew Scotty was going to be writing me, but when Gail (Scotty's mom) mentioned him doing so, I just assumed it was going to be something about prayer or music or something like that. Boy, was I in for a surprise! Like Scotty shared, I had been wedding dress shopping all day on the day the letter showed up, and as a 25 year-old woman who had never myself been married, I had been praying all day that God would soon bring me a godly husband of my own! And then Scotty landed in my mailbox!

It was about 10 o'clock by the time I got home that night and checked the mail. Once inside, when I opened the letter the first thing that caught my attention was how Scotty had drawn my name in bright, neon-colored bubble letters. Still not thinking the letter to be anything romantic, I must admit I was flattered to see that someone had taken the time to make my name look so pretty. However, it was not long before I was beyond flattered and was consumed by the Spirit of God. The anointing on the letter was felt as soon as I opened it, but by the time I realized where Scotty was going, the Holy Ghost had come upon me with indescribable power. I broke in the intensity of His presence, and even though I knew what the letter was going to convey before I even got through the front of the first page, the more I read, the harder I cried and the more real it became. It was so surreal, all the way down to the smallest details. Like everywhere he put a smiley face, I was smiling; everywhere he put "lol," I was laughing; and everywhere he wrote, "Amen," I was "Amening."

By the time I had finished reading the letter, I was bawling crying and convinced that this was God's will for my life. All I could do was thank Jesus for sending me this godly man and for choosing me to be his! Immediately after reading the letter, I knew I had to call Gail. As Scotty's mom and my best friend, I had to tell her that I had gotten the letter and that I was heading over to her house that very instant! Of course, she didn't answer, and so I called Craig (her husband). Still crying, I asked him to put Gail on the phone. When she got on, I told her just that—that I had gotten Scotty's letter and that I was on my way over.

Once over at Craig and Gail's, Gail answered the door, and seeing that I was still crying, she asked if I was okay. I told her I was fine and held out the letter and told her to read it. She asked if I was sure, and I told her that I was and that I needed her to read it. Taking the letter from me, the two of us stepped inside and went over to the living room couch. Sitting on the couch together, Gail let out a big sigh (like, here we go), and began reading the letter aloud. I remember her being wowed by the letter as she read, and two of us crying in awe at what all God had spoken to Scotty. By the time she was finished reading, the same presence of God that had been in my small apartment was flooding her living room. I remember declaring, "This is God's will for my life, and I receive it."

Gail shared with me that she knew what Scotty had put in the letter (though not verbatim), and that she had been anticipating finally finding out if it had all actually been from God or not based on my response. She was elated and in awe at how I had received it, and the two of us rejoiced in the Lord together, thanking Him for His perfect will! There in our sweet embrace of God's precious presence, the song that came to me was, "Little Is Much When God Is In It." I softly began singing the old hymn and continued to do so for weeks on end.

> *"Little is much when God is in it,*
> *Labor not for wealth or fame,*
> *There is a crown, and you can win it,*
> *If you'll go in Jesus' Name."*

I was so excited! I wanted to call Scotty immediately, only Gail broke it to me that I could not call him, but that he would have to call me (prison stuff lol). "Well, can I go see him?" Again, she had to school me about prison policies and such, and how I would have to fill out another visiting application and wait to get approved. Then I could finally go see him, but only on the weekends and only during certain set times. Prison stuff lol! Disappointing as that was, nothing could steal my joy that night, and Gail and I stayed up all night long, just laughing and sharing stories and praising God for all of his wonderful works toward the children of men! Hallelujah!

I (Scotty) knew that Kayla should have been getting my letter Monday night, so when I called my mom on that Tuesday morning, I did so with nervousness and anticipation. I knew there was no way Kayla could get such a letter and not inform my mom about how she took it—for better or worse. I remember when my mom picked up, there was a very sweet peace between us. She quietly and gently told me that Kayla had received my letter, but then just let it linger there. Cliff hanger! I had the very strong unction that it was good news, but obviously needed to hear such confirmation. "Well, what did she say?" I asked.

"She wants you to call her." My mom responded. She did not elaborate too much, wanting Kayla to be able to share with me in detail, but she did tell me that it was good. The two of us wept and praised the Lord together. Hallelujah.

Later that evening, when Kayla was getting off work, I called at our scheduled time. Both of us being in brand-new territory, we were a little shy and awkward that first call. One can only imagine. After that initial conversation, though, we were both open books, talking for hours about anything and everything. It was like we had been cut from the same umbilical cord. Literally. We were and still to this day are transparent with each other.

Within a couple of weeks, I had officially proposed—over the phone. Kayla had still not been able to come up and see me, as we were still waiting on her visiting application to be re-approved. In all actuality, I had felt married to her since the night of my experience, but being on earth, we still have to go through all the little formalities—you know how it is. With this being the case, I didn't think an over the phone proposal was quite formal enough. I mean, come on. Nevertheless, God was persistent in his nudging on that particular phone call, and I reluctantly said, "Yes, Lord."

After singing her a song that was part original, part given to me by a friend, and part on the spot improv, I said, "Kayla Christine Nichols." To which she responded with, "Scott Marshall Davis." At which point, I proceeded to officially ask for her hand in marriage. To this request, she was all sweet and girly and didn't break my heart. Thank you, baby.

From there, I was again reluctant to attach our marriage to the informalness of prison, and so I thought to wait until I was released for the two of us to actually get married. But again, the Holy Ghost was having none of it. "What if the shoe were on the other foot, and she was the one in prison?" He asked. Of course, I would've broke down the gates of the Russian Gulag to put my last name on that woman, and Jesus knew that. So as these thoughts ran through my head, He followed up by asking, "Then why do you cheapen her love for you, thinking that she doesn't feel the exact same way?" He revealed to me that the same Spirit in me was in in her, and therefore the same love and strength that was in me was also in her. Amen.

The prison here only allows weddings to take place in the months of March and September, and since we had missed the boat for March, Kayla and I made plans for that September. As God's will would have it, though, I received the wrong information as far as deadlines for turning in certain paperwork goes, and the iron bars of prison policy prevented us from getting to September. Thinking we had our ducks in a row, we set our sights on the following March, only to encounter more technical difficulties. As it turns out, these hiccups were actually manifestations of God's providential hand at work, and by the time the next September rolled around, my step-dad (more aptly titled as my brother in Christ) had acquired his minister's license for the state of

Missouri, which allowed him to be present at our ceremony. Policy only allows six guests to join the bride and groom, and since Kayla's mom, dad, and grandma were going to be joining my mom, dad, and little sister, this would have left out our brother Craig (who is very near and dear to both of us). God had it all mapped out from the jump, though, and by the time we finally got to September of 2019, Craig was the one asking Kayla and I to recite our vows to one another.

And there you have it, folks—Brother and Sister Scotty Davis. I could not have asked for a sweeter gift. Aside from His very own Spirit, my wife is the greatest thing my Maker could have ever blessed me with. Life on earth is one of joyful struggle, and there is no one else I would rather have by side to aid and assist me on the battlefield. Our marriage has not been perfect, our struggles have been real, and I am still sitting in a cell as I write this. Nevertheless, I have no doubt that our marriage has been one of Divine arrangement, the lessons God has taught us along the way have been invaluable, and through it all the Grace of God has been and ever shall be sufficient in our lives.

If I can add one final word exhortation, may I both encourage and warn you to wait upon the Lord. If you are not yet married, do not rush into a relationship. And most certainly do not jeopardize your walk with God for the sake of carnal enjoyment. If you will wait upon the Lord, not only will you remain in the blessings of Christ Jesus, but you will also end up with the tailored and custom-fit spouse that Creator God has designed and destined specifically for you (if in fact you were called to marry). For those who have been called to marry, the repercussions of marrying the wrong person cannot be overstated, and the blessings of marrying the person God has created for you cannot be accurately measured. Amen, and In Jesus Name, Amen!

Kayla,

1st & Foremost — let everything that hath breath praise the LORD! Praise ye THE LORD!! For Holy He alone hath done wondrous things and He alone is worthy to be praised! Amen!

I know this letter may come as a surprise to you but I pray that it finds you do as well and full of the Holy Ghost. I'm just going to come direct, because that's the direction I feel God leading me in, and from there I can only pray you are responsive to what the Spirit is saying. So 1st I pray in all sincerity that I am in fact being led of God right now (LORD you hear me!) for if not this will all be quite humiliated humiliating though I have learned that one can never to much embrace humility & I suppose that places me in a win, win... :)

So back at the beginning of this year, early January I believe, I had a very very powerful and very real experience in the LORD. Now if I had been in the phone that night and as is our custom we were praying over many different people and about many different things when we began to pray for you, which wasn't at all strange for we've prayed over your life on a number of occasions as have I frequently prayed for you since you were introduced into our lives some time back. But this night was different. As I began to join in praying over you I began to feel some very intense feelings of love well up inside

me, a which I thought to discuss as inappropriate, though they were persistent until we began to lift up other various prayer needs. (And this story is pretty long, but all details I feel are necessary & I'm assured they'll even, if not immediately, some day be greatly appreciated on your end.) And again LORD, if I'm crazy PLEASE stop me now! And with that let us continue. So as soon as I closed out our phone conversation we did so with her saying a powerful prayer over my own life, a specific part which I remember being her praying for God to give me something special & something out of the ordinary that night - something very powerful & something very real! Now fast forward to around eleven o'clock or so that night as I was in bed closing out with my nightly intercessions... Once again none other than yourself came into my mind to pray for & once again with the accompaniment of those blindingly unavoidable feelings & emotions. Only this time as I tried to escape by simply moving on to pray for someone else I felt the LORD pose me this little humungous question, "What if she's the one I've created for you?" Now you've got to understand that up to this point in time I was under the firm belief that God was going to reconcile a relationship between myself & the young lady I'd been with off & on since I was 16, leading up to my arrest - a promise he'd in fact given after I'd fervently prayed for such a gift. (One thing we must always remember though is that if we want something bad enough God will give at times it to us, even if its not His own will or personal desire for us) So,

with all this going on I felt that to even entertain such a question or the feelings that had brought the question about, would be disloyal & saw them as perhaps a need best to my devotion not only to Lauren, but ultimately in my faith for God to bring the seemingly impossible to pass. However it soon became clear that the question was going to be inescapable, and so I dug a little deeper & asked God what the meaning behind all this was. "What if I only promised to reconcile you and Lauren because of how strongly you desired it? & as a Father I felt to hear your desperate plea, but really this (next) is the young lady I've chosen for you from the beginning? Which path would you choose?"

I'll be transparent. I was still quite confused and a bit uncomfortable with this persistent line of questioning & my initial response was to stand on my loyalty to Lauren. Immediately though God reminded me that she was not His actual will for my life, and for me to stand on my "loyalty" would be little more than me standing on my pride. And with this my heart softened, I opened up and I said in my heart, "Ok, Dad, it's just me & You right now, and if all this is real right now then yes, I would choose yours will above all things. I would let go & I would walk in light of your destiny for my life." Now this is where the intensity ramps up lol! As soon as I yielded to what was being presented I was taken to a very supernatural place of ecstasy & bliss that I can only describe as heavenly. Of all the experiences I've had in God none have been more personal & amidst the euphoric emotions that were washing over me I began to receive glimpses of our destiny

together, of our spiritual & physical compatibilities, of our families meshing into one, of our future in music & ministry, and the more I embraced all of this the deeper I was taken. To the point that when I finally stood up out of my bunk I was in such a ~~intense~~ spiritual place that it was humorous to me that I was actually in a physical body... Hallelujah, JESUS, Hallelujah! Ha! Truly we serve an AWESOME God, a FAITHFUL and a RIGHTEOUS & LOVING GOD!!! HALLELUJAH!!!

Paul that's not where the night ended. Once back in bed I was led back to being prostrate on my face in prayer & was once again drawn back into a very intense atmosphere in the spiritual realm, only this time it was one of deep intercession & spiritual warfare over your life. And for the next hour or so I interceded on your behalf with great fervor & against great resistance, to the point that I don't believe I've ever been led to a place of such intense intercession before or after.

When I finally laid my head down to sleep that night, after double checking with God a half a dozen times or so on if everything I'd experienced had been for sure of Him or not I simply felt His sweet peace and very calming assurance. My love for Lauren, a love which I never thought would subside, faded out, replaced by a new & different love for yourself, and from that point on I've been prayerfully waiting & anticipating for God to manifest His sovereign will for our lives. Then a couple days ago it was on my heart to write you & after prayerfully seeking God on the matter, I believed

together, of our spiritual & physical compatibilities, of our families merging into one, of our future in music & ministry, and the more I embraced all of this the deeper I was taken. To the point that when I finally stood up out of my trunk I was in such a ~~____~~ spiritual place that it was humorous to me that I was actually in a physical body... Hallelujah, JESUS. Hallelujah! lol! Truly we serve an AWESOME God, a FAITHFUL and a RIGHTEOUS & LOVING GOD!!! HALLELUJAH!!!

But that's not where the night ended. Once back in bed I was led back to being prostrate on my face in prayer & was once again drawn back into a very intense atmosphere in the spiritual realm, only this time it was one of deep intercession & spiritual warfare over your life. And for the next hour or so I interceded on your behalf with great fervor & against great resistance, to the point that I don't believe I've ever been led to a place of such intense intercession before or after.

When I finally laid my head down to sleep that night after double checking with God a half a dozen times or so if everything I'd experienced had been for sure of Him or not I simply felt His sweet peace and very calming assurance. My love for Lauren, a love which I never thought would subside, faded out, replaced by a new & different love for yourself, and from that point on I've been prayerfully waiting & anticipating for God to manifest His sovereign will for our life. Then a couple days ago it was on my heart to write you & after prayerfully seeking God on the matter, I believed

AFTERWORD

We are living in unprecedented times. The promotion of *alien* ideologies has reached religious proportions on an international level, with the vast majority of the proponents completely clueless to the satanic elements at work. Varying forms of this age-old tactic seem to be as ancient as civilization itself, and its implications cannot be overstated. Add to this devilish agenda the legalization of marijuana and normalization/decriminalization of drug use in general, accompanied by the social media boom linking all walks of life together, and here we are—a very dangerous place to be.

Let me be unmistakably clear, *aliens* are devils. Whether you want to call them devils, or demons, or principalities, or fallen angels, these beings are not friendly, and their ultimate intentions are as wicked as you can imagine. These beings have an intricate, unseen, worldwide network, and have been studying humans since Adam and Eve. They traffic in deception and excel in manipulating vulnerable minds detached from God. From generating visual hallucinations, to making physical appearances, to granting supernatural powers, to speaking through animals, the abilities of these entities are both vast and extreme. Drug and alcohol use enhances the potential for these type of encounters, but it is not always necessary. Any interest or attempt to interact with these beings will likely result in an established connection and quite possibly lead to possession.

Alongside the advent of social media, shows like *Ancient Aliens* have played no small part in accelerating the extraterrestrial narrative. Infamous for taking out of context Bible verses and manipulating them to connect dots with ancient pagan gods (devils), this particular show has presented the masses with a convoluted package of deception. Having once bought into such ideologies, I empathize with how people can be led astray and convinced of all this dot connecting. Satan is no slouch when it comes to the art of deception, and the mind not anchored to the Word of God by the Spirit of God is highly susceptible to being taken by such craftiness. To the learned, it's all quite see-through, but to the unlearned, it's all quite convincing.

This type of indoctrination shows no signs of slowing up, and I encourage all reading this to prayerfully educate yourself further on the matter. If you're still on the fence, seek God for the truth, and He will show it to you. If you understand the truth, be prepared to share it with others. And to all who encounter a being masquerading as an *alien*, rebuke it in the mighty name of Jesus!

FOOTNOTES

1. What Does Acid do to You? The Effects of LSD (Acid). Authored By Erik MacLaren, PhD (https://drugabuse.com/contributors/erik-maclaren/)
2. LSD @ Drugs.com
3. 2013 Report by the Drug Enforcement Administration (DEA)
4. This Is Your Brain On Music by Dr. Daniel J. Levitin

1. 1 Corinthians 5:6
2. Proverbs 29:15
3. 2 Timothy 2:26
4. Philippians 2:13
5. Ephesians 2:2

1. Peter 1:13
2. 1 Peter 5:8

1. E.T. By Katy Perry, produced by Dr. Luke, Max Martin, Ammo, 2011

1. The ankh is an ancient Egyptian symbol used in black magic, especially during sexual rites, symbolizing enteral life.
2. 2 Timothy 2:26
3. First John 4:7
4. Proverbs 10:12
5. Some believe we are only just now starting to see Disney's true colors, but the truth is that *the Mouse* was conceived in wickedness. Walt Disney himself was a thirty-third degree mason, deeply steeped in the occult. Hence, we have an entire empire built on the hellish foundation of *magic*.

Only recently has Disney stepped boldly out of the closet, introducing an openly homosexual couple in their revised casting of *DuckTales* and an unbashful same-sex kissing scene in their latest animated release, *Light year*, but from the beginning, Disney has familiarized innocent children with witches, wizards, and satanic villains. Since their inception, Disney has either attributed the supernatural goodness that belongs to God alone to an act of *magic* or mischaracterized the very idea of "good" altogether. For generations, this mega conglomerate—which also owns ABC, ESPN, Marvel, Pixar, Lucasfilm, Fox Entertainment, National Geographic, Touchstone Pictures, and numerous other companies—has been molding the minds of innocent children with warped ideas of "good" and "evil." We then grow into adults, making decisions for our own children, and what you have is an entity that has subtly and masterfully played a massive role in shaping an entire country's views on things like childhood, fatherhood, motherhood, family, love, marriage, romance, right and wrong, good and evil, fear and courage, and of course, *magic.*

Disney really unsheathed its claws for all to see when the two-ton entertainment tiger roared back against Florida's, *Parental Rights in Education Act.* You would think a bill that protects children third grade and below from being sexually groomed—or sexually anything for that matter—would be supported by a company devoted to children's entertainment, but not when it comes to the beloved Mouse. In an official statement on March 28, 2022, Disney boldly declared, "Florida's HB 1557, also known as the 'Don't Say Gay' bill, should never have been signed into law. Our goal as a company is for this law to be replaced by the legislature or struck down in the courts, and we remain committed to supporting the national and state organizations working to achieve that. We are dedicated to standing up for the rights and safety of LGBTQ+ members of the Disney family, as well as the LGBT+ community in Florida and across the country." Statements like this one make perfect sense, though, with executive producers like Latoya Raveneau proudly trumpeting Disney's "not-at-all secret gay agenda" by "adding queerness" wherever they can.

Over a quarter-century before Disney's "not-at-all secret gay agenda," they were still "adding queerness" wherever they could, only they were using a much subtler method known as "queer coding." The covert strategy of "queer coding" is used to gradually desensitize the viewer to homosexuality and transgenderism. This devilish strategy was executed by homosexual lyricists and artists like Howard Ashman and Andreas Deja. Ashman convinced the animators of *The Little Mermaid* to create the villainous sea witch, Ursula, after the likeness of a popular drag queen of that day called *Divine*. Following suite, Deja would draw such characters as Lefou from *Beauty and the Beast*, Scar from *The Lion King*, and Jafar from *Aladdin* with effeminate mannerisms. Deja's homosexual overtones are also readily visible to the clear-eyed critic in his 1997 animation job in the overtly pagan film *Hercules*.

The philosophy behind "queer coding" was laid out in a November 1987 article in the homosexual magazine, *Guide*, titled "The Overhauling of Straight America." The article reads, *"The first order of business is the desensitization of the American public concerning gays and gay rights,"* wrote Hunter Madsen and Marshall K. Kirk. *"To desensitize the public is to help it view homosexuality with indifference instead of keen emotion. Ideally, we would have straights register differences in sexual preference the way they register different tastes for ice cream or sports games: She likes strawberry, and I like vanilla; he follows baseball, and I follow football. No big deal.*

"At least in the beginning, we are seeking public desensitization and nothing more. We do not need and cannot expect a full appreciation or understanding of homosexuality from the average American. You can forget about trying to persuade the masses that homosexuality is a good thing. But if only you can get them to think that is just another thing, with a shrug of the shoulders, then your battle for legal and social rights is virtually won. And to get to that shoulder-shrug stage, gays as a class must cease to appear mysterious, alien, loathsome and contrary. A large-scale media campaign will be required in order to change the image of gays in America." Who better to help carry it out than Disney?

Aside from "queer coding," let's look at a handful of other sexually deviant subliminal messages that Disney packed in their films during the late 80's and 90's.

The Rescuers: During the scene where the main characters fly down between some skyscrapers on the back of Orville the Albatross, the camera angle tilts up, and when freeze-framed, we get a shot of a bare breasted woman standing in one of the building's windows.

Aladdin: In the scene where Aladdin flies up to Jasmine's balcony on his *magic* carpet, we see him attempting to shoo away her pet tiger. What we don't hear unless we slow the scene down, though, is the endearing Aladdin making the statement, "take your clothes off." Clear as a bell.

The Little Mermaid: Slow down Eric and Ariel's wedding, and what you're assaulted with is the priest presiding over the ceremony sprouting a brief yet definite erection. Look it up for yourself.

The Hunchback of Notre Dame: During the villain, Frollo's disturbingly titled song, "Hellfire," we get a performance otherwise reserved for the strip club as Esmeralda's figure dances erotically in the scene's eerie flames.

The Lion King: After leaving home, there is a starry night scene where after a depressing conversation with his friends, Simba throws himself to the ground causing the dandelions around him to float up into the air. What a perfect opportunity for the creep cartoonist to spell out *SEX* in the floating dandelions. Disney's pathetic defense to this was that they wrote *SFX*, but people mistook the *F* for an *E*. The fact that they admit to having intentionally written anything testifies to the truth of the matter, and only the epitome of narcissism could expect we the peons to believe such an excuse as *SFX*. Keep your ocean front property and your pedophilia as far away from our children as possible.

This brief Disney rundown really is just the tip of an arctic iceberg, and I encourage you do your own independent research. Who knows, maybe you'll write an entire book on the subject.

1. 2 Corinthians 3:17

1. Matthew 19:26

ABOUT THE AUTHOR

Scotty is thirty-two years old, and is nearly eleven years into his twenty-five year prison sentence, where he continues to pursue his passions of reading, writing, song-writing, teaching Bible studies, and helping others. Since being incarcerated, Scotty has also met the love of his life. He and his lovely wife, Kayla, are soon to celebrate their fourth wedding anniversary, and if you were to ask either one of them, they would tell you that even amidst the current circumstances, they have never been happier. Scotty has also been blessed with the continual support of his friends and family, throughout the duration of his incarceration, strengthening the ties that were once frayed.

LSDerailed: *Crashing Into the Occult; Train Wreck Turned Testimony* is Scotty's second published work and is soon to be followed by his first apologetics book, *Tools of The Trade: A Workman's Guide to Defending the Faith*. He has a few other books in mind, as well as a plan to one day record the many songs he has written. We are all praying this to be sooner rather than later, as Scotty is currently appealing his sentence and believes there to be daylight for him, in getting a reduction on the amount of time he will have to serve. In the end however, only the Lord Jesus Christ knows what the future holds in store, and so in the meantime, Scotty continues to grow where he has been planted and do his best to further the Kingdom of God regardless of the circumstances. Amen, and In Jesus Name, Amen!

Scott and Kayla on their wedding day

CONTACT INFO!

Feel free to contact us via email at purposeinthepain2@aol.com and check us out at www.scottysstory.com for book purchases and more info!

Thank You, and may God bless you in Jesus Mighty Name!

Made in United States
Orlando, FL
06 March 2023

30779333R00136